Feeding Our Babies

Exploring Traditions of Breastfeeding and Infant Nutrition

Priya Vincent

Hochland & Hochland Ltd

Published by Hochland & Hochland Ltd, 174a Ashley Road, Hale, Cheshire, WA15 9SF, England.

First edition

ISBN 1-898507-64-3

British Library Cataloguing in Publication Data
A catalogue record for this book is available from the British Library

Printed in Malta by Interprint Ltd

**To the memory of Anne Haggith
My mother who breastfed me**

Contents

Acknowledgements

As I mention in the Introduction, this book was written over a fairly extended period of time during which I had the support and help of many people. I would particularly like to thank all the women who shared with me their birth and breastfeeding experiences. This includes the Shona midwives that I talked to in Zimbabwe and the breastfeeding mothers that I spoke to in Kodaikanal, together with the students in both places who helped me with interviewing and translation. I am very grateful for the help of my friend Ann Salvage and my sister Anna Haggith for carrying out a literature search and photocopying articles that I needed. Living as I do in India their help was invaluable in keeping me in touch with the literature. Finally I would like to thank my three children, Mary, Emma and Rachael, who gave me both the practical experience of infant feeding when they were small and as they got older the understanding and space that I needed to write about it.

Introduction

Having written about traditional midwifery and traditions of birth, writing about traditions of infant feeding seemed a natural next step. While exploring traditions of birth in my travels around Southeast Asia, Africa and India, I inevitably also discussed and collected traditions associated with breastfeeding and infant nutrition. Collating the material and writing this book, however, has taken place over a much longer period than was the case with my previous publications. This was partly because of considerable changes in my own life but also because the nature of the subject matter. It seemed even more diverse than the material I had collected on traditions of birth and took longer to digest and to see how it all fitted together.

Doing research specifically on breastfeeding traditions has taken me to Zimbabwe and to several places in India. Unfortunately I have never had either the time or resources to carry out a 'proper' piece of research capable of corroborating research hypotheses. I used what opportunities I had, however, to talk to both traditional midwives and breastfeeding mothers in traditional communities. I count myself very lucky to have had the opportunity to talk to such women who shared their experiences with me so generously. Any quotations that I give, based upon my own explorations, are to provide the flavour of an idea and to hear another woman talking about her breastfeeding experience, rather than to make a definitive statement about a particular point.

Most of the material on traditions of infant feeding brought together in this book comes from anthropological and sociological work on breastfeeding carried out mainly by academics. In no way can the material presented be seen as comprehensive, although it does contain a range of material from all over the world. There is voluminous literature comprising of statistical studies on breastfeeding which have been carried out in various parts of the world, usually with the intention of providing material useful to breastfeeding programmes. Occasionally such studies do mention breastfeeding traditions, but mostly they are concerned with building up statistical models based on the characteristics of women who do and do not breastfeed. By contrast, most of the research studies that explore traditions of infant feeding in detail are small scale anthropological studies and it is mainly these which are described in this book.

More recently there have been some excellent studies on traditions of breastfeeding which include both data on what mothers say they do, combined with behavioural research which shows what they actually do. Some of these have been described at length as they provide a very rounded picture of both behaviour and beliefs in some traditional communities. There is less research, however, on how women feel about breastfeeding and the meanings it has for them at all levels. Infant feeding is rarely straightforward, and such studies as there are demonstrate the various complex environments in which women feed their infants, together with the intricacies and ambiguities with which they have to contend in order to do it successfully.

Throughout this book I have talked about 'traditional societies' or 'traditional communities' in contrast to the 'west' or 'modern industrial societies'. These are rather loose terms, but for the purpose of this book seemed to me the best way of easily distinguishing between two very different lifestyles. Traditional communities are generally small, with people living in small groups usually based on family ties, growing most of their own food and satisfying most of their needs from their own intellectual and material resources. This is in contrast to modern industrial societies such as the UK, America or Australia, where people live in large urban areas, usually in small nuclear families and who satisfy their material needs by going out to work and spending the money earned on food and goods produced by industrial processes. This is, of course, a somewhat simplistic definition as most countries manifest both kinds of society with urban areas appearing more 'industrial' and 'modern' and groups living in the country appearing more 'traditional'. This is reflected in some of the research studies I describe where there were very different ideas and practices in urban and rural areas of the same country.

Most of the studies mentioned in this book were carried out by one or two researchers, usually with a relatively small group of people at a particular time. Although for convenience I sometimes write 'Mexican women thought that ...', it does not follow that all Mexican women have the same beliefs either now or when the research was carried out. There are differences between individuals and groups in traditional societies just as there are similar differences in western societies. This is particularly the case in communities where women have considerable autonomy with regard to infant feeding and are considered to be the final arbiter concerning what food should be given to their infant and when. In such situations certain mothers may feel quite comfortable in going against taboos with regard to infant feeding, if it seems to them appropriate to do so within their particular situation. The traditions I describe are almost certainly not continuing unchanged as modern ideas, in particular those of modern medicine, are changing them as it changed ours in the west. As some of the research shows, traditional ideas may change in unforeseen ways when they are influenced by modern medicine.

During some of the period of thinking about and writing this book I was breastfeeding my youngest child Rachael and, inevitably, examined my own experience in the light of what I was finding out about other places. It became clear to me that infant feeding, and especially breastfeeding, is not just about getting nutrition into babies. How we do it and the meanings we ascribe to it reflect many things about the environment in which we live. Exploring traditions of breastfeeding in other places can bring into sharper focus what our own behaviour in this area tells us about ourselves and our environment. It also, I believe, helps us to see and appreciate the very diverse ways in which we can and do feed our babies.

PART ONE

BEGINNING, BIRTH AND BREASTFEEDING

CHAPTER ONE

Traditions of Birth and Breastfeeding

The experience of birth and breastfeeding

Breastfeeding, for most women, begins after the birth of their first baby and the experience of breastfeeding is therefore intimately linked with the experience of birth. Although birth as a physical process is the same for all women, the way that we feel and explain it varies considerably. This is also true of breastfeeding. To understand traditions of breastfeeding we need to understand something of the different traditions of birth. For as we give birth, so do we breastfeed.

Before I went to live in Malaysia and started research for my first book on traditions of midwifery (Vincent, 1991) and later birth traditions (Vincent, 1992), my experience of birth was similar to most women giving birth in the west. Pregnancy and birth were not perceived as a normal process but one where medical aid was essential. This was especially so during my first pregnancy when, at age 29, I was deemed 'elderly' and therefore at special risk. The responsibility for finding and dealing with any problems was the doctor's rather than mine and I was not expected to participate in this. Given my age and so-called risk status, I was expected to go to the hospital to give birth, without argument, where I was expected to defer to the medical personnel's idea of what was good for me. I gave birth to my firstborn in the impersonal delivery room of a large hospital with birth attendants that I had never seen before. Throughout the whole process, the focus of the doctors was only on my physical body and on the safe extraction of a healthy baby, with scant attention being paid to my feelings. No-one took seriously my later complaints that I had not been treated with consideration for myself as a person. I had a physically healthy baby and, I was told, should be satisfied with that.

By contrast, when I began travelling around Southeast Asia and talking to mothers and traditional midwives, I found that pregnancy and birth were considered to be a normal part of life. A pregnant woman received advice and care mainly from female relatives and friends and sometimes traditional midwives who supported and guided her. Only if it seemed that she had some special problems would she seek more expert advice, usually from a more powerful traditional practitioner. Pregnancy and birth were perceived as involving emotional and spiritual, as well as physical forces. A pregnant woman, therefore, protected herself not only physically but spiritually with rituals, harnessing positive forces in various ways. Birth took place, sometimes on her own and sometimes with the help of female relatives or traditional midwives, in a place of quiet and seclusion either at home or in a special place set aside for that purpose. The traditional midwife had both the practical expertise derived from helping many women give birth, as well as the ritual expertise necessary to deal with non-physical forces. After birth there was usually a time of ritual exclusion of the mother from normal life to guard against negative forces to which she was especially vulnerable. At the same time, it allowed her to take a break from what was often a physically demanding life during which she could recover from the exertion of birth and establish breastfeeding. Pregnancy and birth were perceived as 'women's business' with the specialized knowledge about pregnancy and birth being found amongst the community of women. Men were, on the whole, not directly involved with birth although in many communities there were various ways in which they might become indirectly involved.

Conversations with traditional midwives in Zimbabwe

Talking to nine traditional midwives in Masvingo, a small town in southern Zimbabwe, showed me very clearly the close relationship between traditions of birth and traditions of breastfeeding. Unlike many developing countries, Zimbabwe actively supports its traditional medical practitioners through ZINATHA, the Zimbabwe Traditional Healers Association. This acts as a central organization for all traditional healers, providing them with certification and making public the extent of their work. It was individuals in the local Masvingo ZINATHA who contacted a number of midwives for me, told them what I was doing and obtained their agreement to talk to me.

Most of the midwives I spoke to lived in rural villages around Masvingo, although one lived on the outskirts of Masvingo and another regularly practised in Masvingo but lived in a village. To help me with the interviews I had the assistance of three university students from the University of Harare who had just finished their undergraduate degrees in social studies. For all of them this was the first piece of 'real' research in which they had been involved. All came from urban backgrounds and what interested me was that they knew almost as little about life in rural Zimbabwe as myself. We visited and spoke to all the midwives in their homes which usually consisted of traditional round houses with thatched roofs. As well as telling me about what they did, they also provided demonstrations and showed me their traditional clothes which they wore while helping women give birth.

In common with most practitioners of any traditional medicine in Zimbabwe, all but one of these midwives were possessed by one or more spirits, from whom came the knowledge to carry out this work. Normally these were spirits of close family members who had died and who had themselves been either a midwife or traditional medical practitioner of some kind. In this way the spiritual healing power was passed from one generation to the next. The midwife called upon this power by allowing herself to become possessed by her spirit when she was helping a mother give birth. It was not the kind of possession where the midwife went unconscious and was not aware of everything that was going on around her. When they described how they became possessed it seemed to me that they were able to be in two different realities at once. As they helped a woman give birth in the physical reality, they were at the same time able to access their helping spirits in another reality which enabled them to do this successfully.

The spiritual possession these midwives were able to undertake and the success of their help to others while possessed was a potent indicator of their power. Within the context of modern medical developments in Zimbabwe these supernatural abilities were gaining importance. The country has a good network of clinics and hospitals based on the western biomedical model to which the majority of people, even in rural areas, have access. These facilities provide competent physical care for mothers and babies during pregnancy and birth, but it was clear that for many mothers this was not sufficient. According to these traditional midwives, providing spiritual protection for pregnant women that was unobtainable in the biomedically oriented hospitals was an increasingly important part of their work.

Unlike traditional midwives in many parts of the world, who are only consulted if there are problems or when labour starts, these midwives were consulted by women as a matter of course during the sixth or seventh month of pregnancy. At the first consultation the midwife consulted her spirit(s) requesting their help. If the spirit felt any incompatibility with the pregnant woman, which indicated that there could be future problems, then the midwife would not accept her. The pregnant woman would then have to find someone else to take her on. This reminded me of similar situations in the west where if a woman is refused a home birth, for example, by one doctor then sometimes it is difficult to find someone else willing to accept her. If one doctor has said the risk is too great, then other doctors tend to concur. I was assured, however, that this situation was quite different. It had to do with compatibility between the midwife's spirit and the pregnant woman and was unrelated to physical risk factors. If a woman was refused by one midwife she would almost certainly be able to find another whose possessing spirit felt that she was compatible. The dangers inherent in taking on a client without spirit acceptance was acknowledged by the increased charges for anyone who came in an emergency. If a client had been accepted by a midwife while she was pregnant then a charge was not normally made and the midwife accepted any gift that was offered. For those who came in an emergency a high charge was made – a cow or the equivalent in money.

Once a woman had been accepted by a midwife, at the first meeting the midwife would feel the baby to make sure that it was in the correct position. If it were felt to be wrong, then herbs would be given which would encourage the baby to go into the right position. In this community there seemed to be little or no reliance on massage as a therapeutic tool and to resolve almost any problems various herbal mixtures would be given, these having magical as well as physical properties. At seven months of pregnancy the mother would be given a mixture of herbs to 'open the way' so that she would give birth easily. Traditionally the mother would then cease to have sexual intercourse until the baby was born. We had some very interesting conversations about the difficulties of doing this within a monogamous marriage which is now more normal amongst the Shona, especially in urban areas. In rural areas, however, men do still have several wives and it was interesting that one of the midwives I spoke to was one of three wives and a family of 21 children. For the majority of women now in monogamous marriages, who did not feel they could refuse their husband's desire for sex, the advice given was to take the herbs to 'open the way' in the morning and then to have a bath before sexual intercourse so 'the way' did not close up again.

It was during the process of labour and birth that the midwife's spiritual power would be used to its maximum. To help a woman give birth she would allow herself to become possessed by her spirit or spirits who would then guide her from moment to moment advising as to the best way of helping the labouring woman. Like most traditional midwives, these women did not have a schedule that they followed for each birth; according to them each birth was different and they needed to be guided by their spirits as to the best way of helping and protecting the woman in each case. To become possessed the midwives needed to dress in special clothes and to hold special items which included a switch made of animal hair. One midwife, dressed in these special clothes, showed me how she helped a woman in labour. She would sit in front of the labouring woman and, by going through each contraction with her, communicate the power of her spirit to help the baby be born. This midwife also showed me a special little stool that she had for her labouring mothers to sit on and it seemed that most women gave birth in some upright position, usually squatting. When the placenta was delivered it was important that the midwife knew which side up it fell down on the floor as this indicated on which side it should be buried depending on the desired sex of the next child.

Once the baby was born all the midwives said they would encourage the mother to breastfeed as soon as possible. In this group there was no reluctance expressed about giving the baby colostrum. One midwife was aware that some groups did not like to feed their babies colostrum but was unable to elaborate on it to any great extent. Within this group breastfeeding was the norm, in the beginning at least, and no one mentioned bottle feeding at all. In my travels around these rural villages I saw no one bottle feeding but many people breastfeeding and even in the cities I saw mothers breastfeeding freely.

Questions were asked about what breastfeeding problems they felt confident about resolving and what they would do for things like sore nipples and insufficient milk. Generally problems were dealt with using the traditional method of rubbing special herbs into small cuts made on the skin of the affected place – in this case the breast. As one midwife explained:

> 'If the mother does not make enough milk I make small cuts on the breast and rub in some medication. I also do this for sore nipples.'

At the same time physical treatment would also be given, especially in the case of insufficient milk. One midwife said she would encourage the mother to eat more peanuts, another that she would give the woman vegetables with a little salt and one said she would give the mother a mixture of herbs called 'dombo'. All the midwives had their own special mixture of 'dombo' herbs which were a kind of tonic which could be given for many different conditions. 'Dombo' would help a baby grow well and could also be given to a mother to build up her strength.

For more serious problems, like breast abscess and mastitis, opinion was divided concerning the extent to which help could and should be given. One midwife said she would immediately refer such a woman to the local clinic or hospital, whereas another midwife said she would try the local herbal remedy first (which she said often worked) only referring to the hospital if this was not successful. All the midwives were aware, however, that any of these problems might have a supernatural cause for which different treatments were needed. This was particularly likely when the baby was refusing to suck properly or if the mother did not seem to have enough milk. As several of the midwives patiently explained to me, only if the cause of the problem was purely physical could it be cured by physical means.

> 'Some problems will be caused by the spirits and in these cases I have to talk to the spirits. The baby can refuse to breastfeed if the mother is a witch or if the grandmother is a witch and interferes. Maybe she is jealous of the baby or something like that even although she may not be aware of it. In some cases the mother or grandmother confesses to witchcraft and that is enough to cure the problem. Sometimes it is enough to give the mother and baby some herbs which will protect them from witchcraft and this will solve the problem.'

Sometimes, however, such problems were caused by the behaviour of adults which went against traditional norms of family behaviour and for which the cure could be quite devastating.

> 'If the baby refuses to breastfeed the problem can be that either the father or mother has been committing adultery. If it is the father he picks a stick outside and gives it to the baby saying, "I am only a man" and the baby starts sucking. If it is the mother she confesses her immorality before her husband and the midwife and this usually leads to divorce.'

> The baby might refuse to breastfeed when the mother has lied about the baby's real father. For the baby to start breastfeeding again the mother has to confess or she can go to a traditional healer for herbs and then the baby can start breastfeeding again.'

The latter treatment had the advantage that it would not lead to divorce. Discussing this later with another traditional healer, he told me of various secret ways that the mother could confess to the healer about her adultery and could thus be cured while not having to confess to her husband and thereby risking divorce. Given the possible devastating consequences of confession, one midwife used the biomedical facilities in what could be described as a creative way to avoid this.

> 'If the baby cannot suck then the mother should confess either to witchcraft or adultery. Because this often leads to divorce I send her to the hospital instead.'

Asked about supplements which were given to the baby, all the midwives thought that when the baby reached six months of age this was early enough. Again it was difficult to tell whether this was traditional practice or whether this was influenced by modern medical ideas. When the baby started to eat solid food he or she would be given 'dombo' usually with maize porridge. If the babies did not flourish on a diet of exclusive breast milk, then 'dombo' would be given either on its own or with porridge while at the same time dealing with any possible spiritual causes for this failure to thrive. Such supplementation of breastfeeding could start as early as two weeks if the baby was not thought to be getting enough breast milk, but it was difficult to say how widespread this practice was.

It was felt that babies should go on breastfeeding for between two and three years after which a number of things would be done to help them stop. Something sour or a special herb could be put on the breasts or the infant was given herbs to help them forget about it. One midwife told me that sometimes a special meal could be prepared for all the children in the village. The child was given some herbs to forget about breastfeeding after which he or she would have the meal with all the other children. Pregnancy was a reason for a mother to stop breastfeeding and the midwives would all advise them to do so otherwise the breastfeeding child might get diarrhoea. If this was impossible for any reason, however, all the midwives had a herbal mixture which would allow the mother to continue breastfeeding without adversely affecting either the breastfeeding infant or the new baby.

In common with all the Shona traditions associated with pregnancy and birth, those relating to breastfeeding recognize the emotional and spiritual, as well as physical, relationship between mother and child. Breastfeeding was not only a physical activity but was also affected by supernatural forces, such as witchcraft, as well as the emotional effects of adult actions when they went against the mores of society. It was interesting that none of these midwives mentioned breastfeeding only in physical terms and, although various physical difficulties were recognized, there was always the possibility that they were caused by emotional or spiritual factors.

In a situation where the overall system of healthcare was biomedically oriented, the capacity to deal with these other forces assumed an increasing importance for breastfeeding mothers in Zimbabwe. Unfortunately I had neither time nor resources to interview breastfeeding mothers in the rural areas where these midwives worked, to find out about their view on the subject and when they sought the help of traditional midwives rather than the biomedical facilities. If the midwives were to be believed, however, they saw themselves as fulfilling an important role for mothers in dealing with these spiritual issues. Everyone I spoke to said that although they did help women give birth, a large part of their work nowadays was involved in dealing with spiritual forces. As far as they were concerned, by using these methods to help women during birth and breastfeeding they were also preserving the essence of the Shona culture.

The bio-cultural nature of breastfeeding

In most of the traditional communities I visited in South East Asia, India and the Shona just described, breastfeeding was the norm and I rarely saw babies being fed from a bottle. Mothers expected to breastfeed and it seemed to me that most mothers did so successfully usually with few of the problems that are associated with breastfeeding in the west. In the many conversations I had with traditional midwives and mothers, I was assured that they had encountered few problems with breastfeeding. Sore nipples, engorgement, mastitis, breast abscess or their local equivalents, were known about but rarely seemed to be experienced. To ensure a good breast milk supply mothers, as a matter of course, took a local prophylactic, such as banana flowers or peanuts soon after birth. From then on most mothers seemed to breastfeed successfully for long periods. It was tempting to assume, as many do, that such women from traditional communities were more tuned into their bodies which made breastfeeding more 'natural' and therefore more inevitable and easier for them to do.

I soon found, however, that the choices such women made about infant feeding were more or less determined by a variety of physical, emotional and cultural ideas and constraints. As one young Indian pregnant mother told me,

> 'Of course I will breastfeed my baby; we all have to here as its too expensive to do anything else.'

The 'choice' to breastfeed for her and the other women in this rural village was made in the context of a difficult economic situation where they could not afford alternatives to breast milk. All seemed very aware that their baby's survival depended on their ability to breastfeed and, not surprisingly, there were a range of traditional remedies to help them do this. Economic pressures meant that if they were unable to breastfeed they could not afford the alternatives and their babies would die. No one in this village mentioned the 'naturalness' of breastfeeding as a reason for doing so. I soon realized that the stereotype of the 'natural' woman from a traditional community who 'instinctively breastfeeds' is no more than just a romantic stereotype which has little or no relationship to reality. In fact, the focus on breastfeeding as a physical activity is very much a preoccupation of western biomedicine. As will be shown in the rest of this book, the traditions associated with breastfeeding take a much wider view and sometimes appear not to support the physical process. For women everywhere breastfeeding has both biological and cultural aspects.

Infant feeding, within traditional communities, often starts with giving the new born pre-lacteal food which is followed by breastfeeding and the traditions that are associated with this are also those that are associated with birth. As birth is both a spiritual and emotional, as well as physical experience, such traditions also relate to these different aspects. As the baby grows, however, other factors become more important in deciding what a baby should eat and in diagnosing and treating problems. This includes traditional ideas about the different stages of a baby's growth and what food is appropriate at each stage, as well as ideas about the nature of the physical body and the best way of keeping it healthy. There is also a range of other factors which impinge either directly or indirectly on the mother and affect the choices she is able to make. This includes such things as the overall economic situation of the community and the family within it and the activities of health workers, governments and commerce. Attitudes towards women, the autonomy which they have, the importance or otherwise of the work of mothering are other factors which can be important. To explore traditions of infant feeding is not just to look at mothers and their children but to look at a mirror of society and its values.

CHAPTER TWO

The Hours after Birth and the Baby's First Food

Pre-lacteal food

Modern research has shown there are good physical reasons for breastfeeding a baby as soon as possible after birth (Kitzinger, 1987). A baby is born with three instinctive reflexes which lead to breastfeeding and are particularly strong in the hours after birth. These are the rooting reflex, which enables a baby to find the nipple, the sucking reflex, which enables the baby to latch on to the breast and start to suck and the swallowing reflex which, when coordinated with the sucking reflex, allows the baby to suckle successfully at the breast. From the mother's point of view, the stimulation on the breast causes the release of oxytocin which contracts the mother's uterus. This, of course, can help with the delivery of the placenta and/or contraction of the uterus which helps to stop bleeding. Research has also shown that if the baby is breastfed soon after birth it leads to longer duration of breastfeeding (Salariya, Easton and Cater, 1978) and that if these are combined with other factors, such as unrestricted contact between mother and baby following delivery, encouragement to feed as frequently and for as long as the baby demands and the withholding of routine additional fluids, breastfeeding is more likely to be successful (RCM, 1988). Thus breastfeeding the baby soon after birth supports the physical process and in the west, at least, appears to lead to more successful breastfeeding.

In many places, however, the traditions related to breastfeeding appear to impede rather than enhance this physical process. Often, breastfeeding does not start for some time after birth varying from a few hours up to four or five days. For many babies in traditional society their first food is of something other than breast milk, which is given for a number of different physical, emotional and spiritual reasons and which can have great symbolic value.

Historically (Radbill, 1981) a wide variety of food has been given to babies prior to breastfeeding. The first food amongst the ancient Israelites, for example, was butter and honey as prophesized by Isaiah of the coming Immanuel, this food representing the ultimate good for mankind. In the Christian Old Testament (book of Ezekial) fine flour and olive oil are also mentioned as food for the child. Amongst the Yurok Indians of California the newborn baby was denied the mother's milk for up to six days as they feared this might lock the baby's jaw. Instead the baby was fed water into which hazel nuts had been rubbed to make it milky. Amongst the natives of Yucatan the newborn baby, prior to breastfeeding, was given a thin gruel made from maize called 'atole' which was mixed with honey. Until the 1750s in Europe and the UK (Fildes, 1986) a wide variety of recommendations were made as to what should be the first food of the newborn. It included colostrum, breast milk from other women, a purge, food, a medicinal substance and combinations of these. There were a large number of different things used as purges when colostrum, the first milk, was not used for this purpose. One of the most popular was butter or oil of sweet almonds combined with something sweet like sugar, honey or syrup, this being very like the butter and honey mentioned above. The aim of the purge was to remove the meconium (a sticky, black substance in the baby's intestines at birth) from the baby's stomach, as well as prevent leprosy, falling sickness and clearing the baby's mouth and stomach by making him cough and vomit.

Similar considerations concerning the need to get rid of the meconium in the baby's stomach were found amongst Kenyan Pokot mothers (O'Dempsey, 1988), who give their babies a pre-lacteal feed consisting of a mixture prepared from hot ash from the fire and water with boiled herbs. This is given using the stem of a castor oil plant as a feeding tube or the horn of an animal. This substance stimulates the baby to vomit any swallowed amniotic fluid. In some cases the bark of an acacia tree can be chewed and the juice given to the baby to induce vomiting. Once either of these things has been given, the baby is blessed by the midwife and given to the mother to start breastfeeding. Discussing this practice with local Village Health Workers the author found that giving such pre-lacteal food to the baby could have disastrous consequences. This included diarrhoea and vomiting, as well as a distended abdomen and the passing of bloody stools, both of which could lead to the baby's death. The author felt this explained the numerous cases of newborns with pneumonia, various infections and dehydration being presented to the local hospital, although this was not investigated in detail.

In Peru (Wellin, 1955) customary practices concerning the baby's first feed were also related to ideas about the stomach and digestion. In this community it is thought that good health results from keeping a 'clean stomach' which is achieved in adult life by regularly taking laxatives – powdered milk of magnesia being a favourite. This promotes a desirable chain reaction in the body which includes a more buoyant circulation of blood and a generally improved body tone. Meconium passed by the newborn is perceived by the mother as evidence that the child has a 'dirty stomach' and that the baby could therefore be open to all sorts of illness if allowed to drink milk on top of this. It is feared that sickness or even death might ensue. It is therefore usual during the first three days of the baby's life not to give any food but to coax the baby to suck bits of cotton dipped in laxative oil to get rid of any meconium that the baby may have swallowed.

Mothers in this community also believe that the infant's ability to suck and swallow is functionally rudimentary just after birth and needs to be stimulated into activity. Sucking on the oil-soaked cotton is considered a necessary trial run for arousing the sucking reflex needed to suck breast milk. Milk is also regarded as 'too strong' for the delicate newborn and the three days during which the baby sucks this oil prepares the baby's body for the 'shock' of milk. The newborn is perceived as still essentially embryonic and not yet fully formed and requiring maternal aid to perfect physical formation. As well as being responsible for getting the sucking reflex to work properly, mothers also mould their baby's head to expedite closing of the fontanelle and put a band around the baby's stomach so that it does not float free. Limbs are straightened with swaddling and massage.

Similar ideas were expressed in Guatemala (Solien de Gonzalez, 1963), where general beliefs about the stomach and how to avoid sickness are also related to the initial food that a baby might receive. Babies are thought to be born with worms in their stomachs and so long as the worms are not disturbed it is believed that they remain quietly in the body and do not cause problems. If the babies eat something that bothers them, however, the worms start moving about and cause pain. If they are active and numerous enough they can cause diarrhoea. At the time this research was carried out, however, this belief was not widespread although sometimes a newborn baby would be given cooking oil immediately after birth to clean out and get rid of any worms which might be active in the stomach. The majority of mothers, apart from a few who offered their babies spoonfuls of boiled sweetened water, gave their babies nothing until the breast milk came in from two to four days after birth.

The giving of various kinds of pre-lacteal food is widespread in Pakistan as was shown in a study carried out there (Ashraf, 1993). All the newborns received some kind of pre-lacteal food with just over a half (53 per cent) being given herb water, usually a mixture of aniseed, cardamom and rose. A third (31.5 per cent) were given honey and a smaller proportion (23 per cent) sugar water. Honey was most popular amongst those mothers in urban areas who could most easily afford it, while those from rural areas preferred the cheaper herb water. Economic status was an indicator of other differences concerning the other kinds of food given to babies at this time. The more upper class mothers gave their babies fresh animal milk or formula which was true of only a small percentage (ten per cent and seven per cent) of poorer mothers in the village and city. There were also differences in how the first feed was given with those in the upper middle classes tending to use a bottle, while poorer mother used their hands or a spoon. Those in the village were more likely to use a wick or dropper. This food was believed to act as a laxative to facilitate rapid evacuation of the meconium.

Similarly in India, where various research studies (Katiyar, 1981 and Chandrashekar, 1985) found that milk of various sorts and glucose or honey water was a frequently given pre-lacteal feed. Mothers in wealthier urban areas were more likely to use cow's milk, while those in the poorer urban areas and those in rural communities were more likely to use sugar/honey water and goats milk. In these latter communities this first food was given within four to six hours of birth, while in the urban group this was delayed to six to eight hours after birth. Taking the sample as a whole, less than five per cent of infants were given a first feed given within one hour of birth.

A detailed ethnographic account of infant feeding practices in Mithila in northern India (Reissland and Burghart, 1988) provides an interesting insight into the cultural beliefs and practices which support the giving of various kinds of pre-lacteal food. In this community, as in many places in India, the first food given between four and 12 hours after birth is sweetened liquid on a cotton twist. Honey is the traditionally preferred sweetener, but the cost and availability of this was beyond the financial reach of most of the women in the sample. Initially the purpose of the custom was to wish the baby a sweet life and the person who feeds the baby with this first food is considered to be impressing her moral character upon the child. Thus the choice of the person to do this is most important. At the same time the importance of the female relatives on the father's side of the family is emphasized as the person chosen for this first feeding is usually initiated by the child's father's sister, the father's mother or the father's elder brother's wife.

Shortly after this first wishful feed, the baby is offered its first milk. Traditionally this was goat's milk but mothers could not explain why goat's milk is considered better than other kinds of animal milk. Buffalo milk, for example, is considered to be too fatty and also to contain the supposed characteristics of the dairymen – dim wittedness and a propensity to alcoholism – which could be passed on to the baby. The local Vaidya (traditional doctor), however, explained that in the Indian Ayurvedic traditional medical system, milk has a medicinal value and the most beneficial of all milk is that of the goat. This animal grazes freely and eats things which are both pure and impure, the latter being destroyed by the fire of the goat's digestion. This leaves behind the full range of pure things which passes into the milk. The goat's milk, being pure and faultless, is thereby empowered to destroy illness caused by all the factors which in the Ayurvedic system are thought to cause illness. Giving goat's milk to the newborn, therefore, destroys any fault or illness which might have been passed to the child through the mother. Despite this ideal, goat's milk was not easily available in this area and usually the baby was given either warmed cow's milk or the milk of a wet nurse. In the latter case the woman preferably came from the same courtyard as the mother as she was the only person who was deemed eligible to stand in for the mother until her own milk was ready.

My experience in India suggests that many mothers now do feed their babies colostrum soon after birth but this has not stopped the tradition of the wishful feed which may, depending on where the baby was born, be given either soon after birth or when the baby comes home from hospital. Talking to breastfeeding mothers in Kodaikanal in Southern India, one mother told me of how her daughter was given a wishful feed of honey by her father. Ruefully she told me,

> 'The person who gives this feed is supposed to impress their character on the child, but I don't think it works. My father is so quiet and calm and my daughter has turned out quite the opposite!'

As in the west, and with more babies being born in hospital, the amount and type of pre-lacteal feeds can depend very much on hospital policies and personnel. A study in Kannada in India found that babies born to mothers who had a caesarean or who were not roomed-in were far more likely to receive a pre-lacteal feed of glucose than those whose babies were born vaginally and/or were rooming-in. Similarly in Thailand (Jackson, 1992) where research showed that nearly all the babies in the sample (of which only 1.8 per cent had been born at home) had received some form of pre-lacteal feed while in the hospital nursery before being taken to their mothers. In this group 27 per cent did not know whether their babies received any pre-lacteal food or not. It should be noted that until very recently it was hospital policy in Britain to give pre-lacteal feeds either of sugar water or boiled water to all newborns. I remember after the birth of my first daughter – only 20 years ago – having to be very insistent that she not be given anything other than my breast milk.

Rituals for breastfeeding

Rituals are an important way of harnessing positive powers for any important activity or event and, in traditional communities, are often more of an integral part of life than they are in the west. During pregnancy and birth there are a wide range of rituals which can be used both as a prophylactic to ensure an easy birth and as a way of coping with any problems or difficulties. Many such rituals include those which are specifically for ensuring that a new mother has a good supply of nourishing milk for the newborn, this being particularly important after the birth of the first baby. Often such rituals use 'sympathetic magic' which is the use of (usually natural) items in the ritual which have characteristics similar to the situation that one wants to invoke.

In the Philippines (Fernandez and Guthrie, 1984), there is a ritual called 'lihi' which denotes 'the first time' and is a general reference to rituals which mark the passage of an individual from one developmental stage to another. In this context the birth of the firstborn is of crucial importance. How this pregnancy and birth is conducted has implications for how easy or difficult future pregnancies and births are likely to be, as well as whether the mother will produce enough breast milk. For this reason the rituals surrounding the first birth may be especially elaborate and carried out with greater care than for subsequent births. Immediately after disposal of the placenta, a ritual consisting of two parts is performed. First, the mother drinks a chocolate drink to make the milk sweet. To ensure whiteness and density of breast milk this chocolate drink may also contain the sap of an unripe papaya. The mother takes the fruit in her cupped hands and pinches it three times with her thumb nails, catching the juice in the chocolate drink. Additional things which may be added to the drink include dried and powdered placenta of cat (this promotes speedy recovery of the mother as cats do not bleed after giving birth), hermit crab (for resilience) and scrapings from the central housepost (to give strength – if this post collapses so does the house). The second part of the ritual consists of the ritual brushing of the mother with leaves taken from sugar cane, papaya or another plant that exudes a milky substance from its branches when cut. The 'hilot' (traditional midwife) takes the leaves in her hand and brushes the mother three times, once on each side of the body, in the region under the armpit, once between the breasts and once between breast and womb while the mother drinks the chocolate.

Another ritual is performed at the mother's first bath. Like many communities in this part of the world it is thought unwise for the mother to bathe too soon after birth as bathing could close up her womb and the blood will not be able to flow out properly. This could cause either a tumour, a local condition called 'bughat' in which the mother becomes weak and unwell, or a relapse which could lead to the mother becoming very weak with diminution and eventual disappearance of her breast milk. Various leaves are used in the bath and although there is wide variation, there is usually one which when boiled gives a milky appearance to the water. When the mother is ready a knife is fired until red hot and this is plunged into the bath after which the mother steps on the blade and pours water over herself three times. A general belief in many parts of the world is that metal, especially steel, protects against bad spirits. In this case the ritual makes the mother 'as strong as tempered steel' for all the tasks she will have to undertake as a mother. In a more elaborate ritual the newly delivered mother may also have to perform other tasks such as uprooting weeds and winnowing, all of which have symbolic value in her new status as a mother. These two rituals are first to enhance the quality of the breast milk and secondly to strengthen the mother and thus avoid misfortune.

In Mexico (Millard and Graham, 1984), sweat baths are taken after giving birth and are considered crucial to the production of good breast milk. During a sweat bath the mother's breast milk, which in its natural form is considered to have qualities that are animalistic, contaminating and possibly perverting, is transformed into a cooked food that is ideal for infants. One way that mothers demonstrate their concern for their infants is by regularly taking sweat baths. At the same time, taking a sweat bath gives women an opportunity for intense and regular interaction with other women and an opportunity for breastfeeding women to consult each other while having a rest.

In Mithila (Reissland and Burghart, 1988) there is considerable concern that breast milk could be spoiled by witches who would affect the breast in a way which causes the baby to lose interest in feeding. One way of dealing with this is to wash the breasts with water which is then poured at a crossroads to be taken away by an unlucky traveller. After returning from carrying out this activity, the mother spits on her breasts before breastfeeding her baby. Spitting is a common prophylactic against witches and some women always do this as a precautionary measure prior to feeding their baby. Witches can also act by sending ghosts and other superhuman beings to drink the mother's milk while she is asleep. When she wakes up and tries to feed her child there is hardly any milk left. A poisonous snake might also wrap itself around the mother's waist and take her milk, and with a withering glance cause her milk to dry up completely. It is popularly thought that such witches are childless or infertile women who long for children. Their personal discontent is dangerous, for in their envy of happy childbearing women they remove, by subtle means, the souls of young children. Since the glance of a witch is thought to be particularly potent while the baby is nursing, the mother should cover the child's face and her breast while breastfeeding.

Talking about birth and breastfeeding with mothers from a community near Delhi, Janet Chawla (1994) was told about a ceremony that many of the women performed, with the help of their daughters-in-law or 'nanad', prior to the first breastfeed. It is common amongst these women to give the baby 'gur', honey or 'janam ghutti' for the first two or three days after birth. During this time the milk, or colostrum, is pressed out and put into the ashes of the fire. Various explanations are given for this – that the milk is stagnant and so should not be fed to the baby and that if the expressed milk is allowed to fall on the earth the spirits would smell it. This could lead to many negative effects, in particular the drying up of the mother's milk. Once the mother is ready to begin breastfeeding the nanad washes the mother's breasts, after which the baby starts to breastfeed. The nanad is given gifts for her part in this ceremony which, if they are very valuable, she normally returns. Janet Chawla thinks that once this ritual was carried out by the Dai (traditional midwife) who has now been superseded by nanad. Various explanations have been put forward to explain this. As the daughter of the house and the recipient of the family's affections she has been superseded by the newborn. Her feelings of exclusion and jealousy towards the new baby are preempted by her centrality in this ritual after birth. Another explanation is that by the ritual receiving of gifts for her role in this ceremony, the dangers to mother and child are ritually transferred to the nanad. Thus mothers are given magical protection to ensure trouble-free breastfeeding through the water which the nanad uses to ritually wash away any potential problems.

The first breastfeed

In communities where colostrum is not given to babies, it may be some time before the newborn receives the first breastfeed. In Pakistan (Ashraf et al, 1993), for instance, only 15 per cent of all newborns received breast milk within 24 hours of birth. Information was obtained from four groups of mothers in urban and rural communities which showed considerable differences in when breast milk was first given to the newborn. At 48 hours, 65 per cent of babies in the periurban slum and 45 per cent of those in the village had not received a first breastfeed. This probably arose from the greater likelihood that mothers took a more traditional view of colostrum and did not want to feed it to their babies. At 72 hours, 82 per cent of these infants had started breastfeeding. In the upper middle class, ten per cent of babies were still waiting for their first breastfeed at 96 hours. No explanation was given for this long wait, but it may have been because in this group exclusive breastfeeding was not carried out by anyone, although 86 per cent of infants were receiving some breast milk at the age of one month.

In Peru (Wellin, 1955), the time when the first breastfeed should take place is – like the giving of pre-lacteal feeds – determined by general ideas about the baby's body and its digestion. It is thought that the newborn's body is underdeveloped and not ready for milk just after birth so breastfeeding is generally started on the third day when the milk comes into the breasts. Although the mother feeds the child on demand, she tries to underfeed at each nursing for the first few days. This is part of a gradual initiation into breastfeeding, bridging the change from pre-lacteal feeds of oil to breast milk. It is only when the mother feels that the baby has got used to and can digest the milk properly that unrestricted suckling is permitted. This is expected to happen after a week or so.

Hospital routines are a very potent factor relating to the timing of the first breastfeed for the increasing numbers of women in developing countries who give birth in hospital. Ironically, while hospital personnel may be influenced by positive ideas about the benefits of colostrum and early initiation of breastfeeding, hospital routine all too often interferes with this. The negative influence of hospitals and clinics was shown in the already mentioned research study in Thailand (Jackson, 1992). Immediately after birth newborns were automatically taken to a nursery for a period of time and because of this initial separation, only 38 per cent of mothers initiated breastfeeding within 24 hours. Despite this, however, nearly three quarters (72 per cent) of mothers fed their babies colostrum and within three days 90 per cent of mothers were breastfeeding.

The influence of different hospital policies on the first breastfeed were evident in research carried out in India (Chandrashekar, 1985). More than half the babies born in hospital who roomed-in with the mother were breastfed within 24 hours of delivery, compared to 33 per cent of non-roomed-in babies. The type of birth was also important as only 14 per cent of newborns born by caesarean, as opposed to 58 per cent of those born vaginally, were breastfed within 24 hours. Almost equal numbers of mothers from four educational groups thought that the first breastfeed should be within 24 hours. Just over one third (35 per cent) of mothers thought that breast milk should be the first feed showing that traditional ideas about colostrum were gradually changing, probably mostly amongst the educated elite. Similar findings were shown in Indonesia (Hull, Thapa and Pratomo, 1990), where it was found that while most babies (61 per cent) began suckling within 12 hours of birth, only seven per cent started within one hour of delivery. Of the 18 per cent who were delayed beyond 24 hours, the majority of these were non-normal deliveries.

The positive influence of a clinic on breastfeeding was demonstrated in a study carried out in Mali (Dettwyler, 1987). Clinic personnel had ample opportunity to influence breastfeeding and did so in a very positive way. The baby was handed to the mother immediately after birth and some babies had their first feed very soon afterwards. Most were breastfeeding within a few hours of birth. No posters advertising formula were in the clinic and bottle feeding was not suggested. The effect of hospital policies on the initiation of breastfeeding is, of course, recognized in the 'Baby Friendly Hospital' initiative where hospitals are encouraged, like this clinic, to organize themselves in ways which will promote breastfeeding.

As previously discussed, in the hours immediately after birth, both mother and baby are physically in a state that is particularly conducive to beginning breastfeeding. Yet, as we have seen, in traditional communities there can be considerable interference in this physical state during the hours and days after birth. In the west, such interference tends to lead to both less initiation and duration of breastfeeding, but in traditional communities it seems to have much less effect. This supports the results of other modern studies which show that although in the period immediately after birth there is a strong physical imperative for breastfeeding, there is not a 'critical period' for the first feed in terms of breastfeeding success. In other words if breastfeeding does not take place immediately after birth, it does not follow that the mother will not be able to breastfeed successfully. This, of course, is amply demonstrated by those few mothers who breastfeed without ever having given birth. In fact it is difficult to separate the effects of early suckling per se from the effects of other early mother–baby interactions (Enkin, Keirse, Renfrew and Neilson, 1996). Early suckling is only one factor in a web of connected factors (continuous contact between mother and baby, unrestricted suckling to name but two) which are necessary for successful breastfeeding. Its importance as a predictor of breastfeeding success varies in different cultural settings.

The giving of pre-lacteal food in traditional communities is part of a wider system of beliefs concerning the nature of the first milk, colostrum, and whether or not it should be given to the newborn. Mothers do not expect to feed their newborns immediately after birth but to wait until their milk comes in and then to breastfeed for long periods. They see other mothers doing the same thing and it seems that these strong cultural expectations are enough to overcome the traditions which disrupt the physical process of breastfeeding immediately after birth. It is also possible that the traditions of exclusion, where mothers and their newborns are isolated together from the rest of the community for a period after birth, extends the period during which a mother and newborn are especially tuned in to each other. Perhaps this also helps overcome the initial disruptions of the physical process of breastfeeding immediately after birth.

CHAPTER THREE

Feeding Ourselves and Feeding Our Babies

Exclusion after birth and the support of breastfeeding

In many, if not most, traditional societies around the world there is usually an exclusion period after birth when the mother is restricted in various ways as regards the food she should eat and what she is able to do. Frequently the mother is considered to be in a delicate state after the exertion of giving birth, as well as ritually unclean, which makes her prey to negative influences which can be physical, emotional or spiritual. She is thus in need of special care and attention, which includes being looked after physically, and protected against evil influences with a variety of ritual observances. It is considered very important for the health of both mother and baby that this period is observed, and even very poor families will do all they can to make sure that it happens, even if they cannot manage to do so for the full period that is traditionally prescribed. A large part of the ritual exclusion is concerned with making sure that the mother gets enough of the right food both for herself and her baby. For many mothers this may be one of the few times in their lives when they have sufficient food which they have not had to cook. Usually the food is of a special sort which is believed to strengthen her body and counteract any weakening influences immediately after birth. Often she will be given special food thought to be particularly helpful for producing sufficient breast milk.

In Yemen (Berkerleg, 1991), for instance, women are expected to remain confined to the house for at least 40 days which is the ritual period laid down in the Koran. During this period mother and child are considered very vulnerable and will be surrounded by protective charms and devices, such as copies of the Koran texts on the wall and bunches of pungent smelling rue pinned to the mother and child's clothing. All these things are meant to counter voluntary or involuntary envy which may come from other women and which might harm the child. Yemeni mothers consider this to be a time of rest and privilege during which they are given special food which includes chicken, spiced coffee and a special drink called 'gishr' to help her regain her strength.

After the 40 days seclusion, a religious ceremony of considerable formality called 'Maulid' is performed. This is an important ritual carried out by and for women. The baby is brought in, perfume is sprinkled over everybody and religious readings begin. At a set point everyone holds out their hands in supplication and later pass hands over baby, singing Koranic verses. After this ceremony has taken place the mother can then undertake a ritual cleansing. This is carried out at the hammam where there is a fixed pattern of steaming and washing which she undergoes. Only after this is she able to resume her normal work within the house.

In Mexico (Skeel and Good, 1988) there is also an exclusion period of 40 days following birth called 'La Cuarentena'/'Dieta'. The mother does no hard work, has no sexual relations and takes baths in which herbs have been steeped and which are thought to be particularly good for her body at this time. She has a special drink called 'atole' which consists of milk, sugar and either oatmeal or cornmeal and this together with chicken soup is drunk in order to produce more breast milk. An important thing that she must do during this time is to stay contented and especially not to get angry or frightened as this could spoil her milk. Her family are expected to help her achieve this.

In Guatemala (Solien de Gonzalez, 1963), the mother is not bathed and stays in bed for three days, during which she takes aspirin for pain and has her abdomen bathed and massaged with oil and bound in cloths. She eats only soup made of hen (not cock) and white bread with sweetened coffee. Chocolate is considered an ideal drink for her at this time. After eight days the mother is able to have a bath in warm water. The ideal period for the mother to stay in her house is thought to be 40 days, but this could rarely be achieved by the mothers in this study as economic and other pressures meant they had to resume their ordinary life as soon as possible.

The African Pokot (O'Dempsey, 1988) woman is restricted after birth in ways similar to those when she is menstruating. For the first few days after birth she must not touch anything except her clothes and the baby. She must not touch any food and must be fed by the women attending her or feed herself using a stick. She does not go out in public and wears her 'kolika', which is the skin cloak she received and wore during her initiation. After four days she has a ritual bath and another one after one more week which includes a ceremony called 'lapow'. Only after this is the mother able to eat with her own hands and be seen in public (the newly delivered mother is decorated to show she has just been delivered and can be avoided by people whose shadows are dangerous). There are a number of food taboos which she observed during pregnancy which still operate throughout this time. One of the most important of these is that she must not drink water or she may suffer backache and/or die. Interestingly, the researcher found that mothers who gave birth in hospital thought that the injection (ergometrine) they received there after birth abolished the harmful affects of water and allowed the mother to ignore this taboo and some other restrictions. This had both positive and negative effects. Although it meant newly delivered woman were somewhat less restricted, it also meant that in some cases women were not looked after or rested as much as they needed after birth. When the lochia has finished, the time of semi seclusion is over and she is allowed to handle food and cook for men. Feasts are held to celebrate this return to normal life but mothers are expected to stay constantly with their babies for three months; obtaining help from neighbours with household chores. They continue to be subject to various food taboos, in particular not drinking fermented milk or meat soup which is thought to go straight to the baby and be bad for him or her.

In the semi-westernized Chinese Sarawak society (Tieh Hee Hai Guan Koh, 1981), newly delivered mothers are confined to their houses for 30 days. During this time a woman is not allowed to go outdoors, expose herself to a breeze or the fan, wash her hair (so she does not suffer from headaches, 'wind in the head', later in life), take a bath, touch cold water or do heavy work. All that a new mother is expected to do is eat, sleep and look after the baby while a relative or servant looks after the mother which includes preparing special food for her. The mother's diet during this period consists of rice, whole chickens (average number 17) stewed in white wine or brandy, pig's intestines, or kidneys and also chicken cooked in 'Kachan ma', which are very strong spices. She does not eat seafood as fish and crabs, particularly, are considered toxic for the wounds sustained during delivery. Other food which she avoids includes sour fruit and vegetables like oranges, pineapples and cabbage, all of which are considered too cool for the baby who might get diarrhoea if the mother eats these things. The traditional explanation for this is that after giving birth the mother has an excess of 'yin' energy within her body, which means that she is in an over passive and receptive condition. This, together with the fact that the pores of the woman are open for 30 days after the delivery, means that she is very vulnerable to both 'cold' (which is considered a kind of energy capable of causing various diseases as well as actual cold) and evil spirits. Hence the need for the mother to be secluded to stop cold air and evil spirits entering and eating 'hot' foods to counteract these effects.

The Indochinese (Hull et al., 1990) have similar beliefs about the time immediately after birth being a time of vulnerability for the mother who is believed to lose 'vital energy and heat' and to enter into a 'cold state'. This is counteracted by keeping her warm and confined for at least one month in a room that is sealed against wind and drafts. The new mother is fed chicken and other food which is considered hot. She receives steam baths and is kept very warm with a piece of burning charcoal, a process known as 'mother roasting' which is very widespread throughout south-east Asia.

In Mithila, India (Reissland and Burghart, 1988), the time immediately after birth is a time of ritual isolation. At the culmination of labour the child 'takes' birth and the mother becomes defiled by blood and afterbirth. The immediate concern as far as the mother is concerned is that the stale blood in the womb should be completely expelled with massage (which most women in the study couldn't afford) and heating tonics. If this is not done it is thought that the stagnant blood could rise in the body, contaminating the mother's fresh blood, causing illness in the mother and contaminating the breast milk and therefore the child. In dire circumstances, it could also cause the production of breast milk to stop altogether. In the week following birth, women refer to the birth passage as a sore or abscess which had been opened to expel the baby and which must now heal and close. Until this has happened a woman feels immodest and various squatting positions are used to promote closure. During the time when her body is open in this way, a mother remains vulnerable to malevolent spirits which can possess her womb and cause madness or sterility. In order not to court such risks she stays in the birth room for six days while ritual prophylactics guard the door; windows are kept closed to deter entry by wind borne illnesses. In addition certain foods are not eaten which might impede the healing of the sore. All this is of equal importance for the baby as the physical qualities of the taboo foods are transferred through the milk to the baby, thereby preventing the umbilical stump from healing.

One of the foods that the mother consumes just after birth is 'halwa' (thought of as a 'heating' food) which combats the cold state of her body immediately after birth. This is prepared from wheat semolina to which mustard oil and heating substances such as black peppercorns and ginger have been added. It helps to bring in the 'real' milk, although the 'full milk' is not thought to come for another two or three months. During this period there is a double preoccupation both with the state of the mother's body and with the production of breast milk. There is concern to establish a regular abundant flow but at the same time her milk has to be protected from deleterious postpartum effects. The ability to do this is linked to the mother's nutritional status and hence the concern that the mother regains her appetite and observes a balanced diet, consisting of readily digested foods. During the first week postpartum a tonic made of 32 ingredients is prepared and taken, each item being a specific against a particular postpartum complaint. In addition to this tonic, food items such as sago and a special type of lentil are thought to be beneficial. Recovery from the birth is linked to the production of 'full' milk which sometimes does not appear for several months. Few mothers think that the sucking action of the baby stimulates the milk flow, although at the same time, they consider it important that the milk continues to flow otherwise it goes stale or bad and curdles, making the baby ill. Forty days after giving birth the purity of the mother is considered restored and she resumes a normal life, reintegration being symbolized by her drawing water from the well.

In a study carried out in Bangladesh by the Save the Children Fund, it was found that the postnatal period was one of the few times when a woman was given special food and was allowed to eat as much as she wanted. Generally in this area women were malnourished, this being exacerbated during pregnancy by the fact that they would not eat too much to avoid having a baby that was too large – which was probably a reasonable thing to do given their general malnourished state and the lack of medical facilities should there be problems during birth. Once she has given birth, however, and depending on her caste, a ritual meal is given to the mother on either the 6th, 9th or 30th day after giving birth. This meal contains many nutritious foods, especially fish. First the mother is fed by one of her female relatives and then, in contrast to the time of pregnancy, she is encouraged to eat as much as she can. As this celebration is omitted if the baby dies soon after birth, the researcher thought that it is probably supposed to stimulate milk production. The ritual conveys interesting ideas about the mother's need to eat nutritious food but it is a once only affair and the quality and quantity of food is not repeated.

A time of seclusion for mother and child immediately after birth is an ideal time for the establishment of breastfeeding providing as it does both privacy and support for the mother, together with constant contact between mother and newborn. It could be one of the factors which counters the sometimes considerable gap between birth and breastfeeding, as it enables mother's to remain 'tuned in' to their babies even though they may not be breastfeeding. As previously mentioned, in some communities such as that described in Mithila, mothers are not expected to bond with their newborns immediately after birth and this time of exclusion enables them to regain their strength so that they are able to do so. This could be more necessary in communities where women are malnourished and anaemic and for whom the exertion of giving birth makes them more physically weak. As mentioned before, research on western mothers shows that breastfeeding soon after birth is associated with longer breastfeeding duration. Perhaps this is because without a time of exclusion after birth mothers get 'tuned out' from their babies more quickly so that breastfeeding has to happen soon after birth if it is to happen at all. If mothers are unable to make a close connection with their newborn immediately after birth, the environment in which they spend the hours and days after birth may be such that it is difficult to do later on.

It is possible, however, for such an exclusion period to have a deleterious effects on breastfeeding duration when this happens to women who work in a modern economy. In Malaysia, for instance, a woman is allowed 44 days leave from work after giving birth, this 44 days being the traditional time after which a mother was expected to return to normal life. When 'normal life' consisted in working in the house and fields, this was congruent with continuing breastfeeding, but when this consists of the kind of work normal in an industrial society, it is not. Several times I came across the erroneous belief that either it was only possible to breastfeed for 44 days or that this was the ideal breastfeeding period even when a mother was in a situation where she could breastfeed for longer.

Eating to breastfeed

Do we need to eat special things in order to breastfeed? Nowadays the general advice is to eat a healthy diet – which in western biomedical terms means the right balance of carbohydrate, protein and fat with sufficient vitamins and minerals. Provided one has eaten in a healthy way during pregnancy, then it is generally agreed that unless there are special circumstances, no special food is necessary for breastfeeding provided one eats enough. In traditional societies, however, there are usually one or more types of food which are thought to be particularly good for stimulating the production of breast milk. Usually women will be given these as a matter of course during the exclusion period and they may continue to eat them during the rest of the breastfeeding period, especially if they feels that her milk supply is diminishing.

According to Fildes (1986), during the 17th and 18th century in Europe there were various traditional remedies for improving the milk supply which could be taken. They included more than 65 ingredients although there were some that were thought to be particularly powerful. These included fennel seed or root, aniseed, powdered crystal, parts of the body or products from cows which included powered udders hoofs and/or broth made from the tongue, powdered earthworms and dill, parsnip, and lettuce. Many things were considered good for breast milk according to the rules of 'sympathetic magic', whereby anything that was moist, white in colour or had milky juice in it was considered good for breast milk production. Thus milk thistle and milk stones were thought to aid lactation. The ingestion of different parts of the cow was thought to be good because it was a prolific milk producer. This is still very much the case today where I live in India and in many other traditional communities.

Theories about the effect of different types of food on the body may also be important. In Peru (Wellin, 1955), for instance, it is thought that some foods are 'hot' and some 'cold', this being related to their inherent qualities and effect on the body rather than temperature. A distinction is also made between 'light' and 'heavy' food. Items with high starch and low water content are described as 'heavy' and are thought to have perverse digestive and stomach fouling properties. Light foods are 'not heavy' and have indifferent nourishment value. Adjusting the diet in various ways is a preventive medicine for those in a delicate state which is intermediate between health and illness and includes pregnant and breastfeeding mothers. During this time it is generally felt that 'hot' foods should be avoided, as they aggravate heartburn and there is always the possibility that the heat could activate the uterus leading to abortion or premature labour. While breastfeeding, the consumption of hot foods transmits a hot quality to the breast milk which can be too great a stimulant for the infant. Some cold foods such as pork and watermelon are considered too cold to be eaten by a breastfeeding mother and others such as fish, leafy vegetables and fruit should be taken only in small quantities and at midday when the sun's heat is at its maximum and mitigates the cold effects. Cold is profoundly feared and is thought to lodge in the organism of mother or child and wreak harm long after it has entered the body.

As far as 'heavy' foods are concerned, it is thought that these should be taken only in moderation. Eggs and certain fruit are completely avoided and others such as potatoes, other tubers and all meat is consumed only at midday. Such foods contribute to a dirty stomach (one of the main precursors of illnesses of various sorts) and make the supply of breast milk sluggish. During pregnancy such food might give the mother an inordinately heavy weight gain which not only makes her ugly in the eyes of others but can also lead to a difficult labour. Mothers prefer to give birth to a small rather than a large baby and are ashamed of too large a baby which is considered ugly. During pregnancy, however, mothers are encouraged to indulge in any unexpected food fancies which seemed to be geared to things that do not violate these restrictions such as raisins, prunes, candies and pastries. It is also recommended that breastfeeding mothers drink tea regularly in the evening in the belief that by morning it helps to produce an ample supply of breast milk. During both pregnancy and breastfeeding mothers consume less meat, eggs, and fresh fruit and vegetables than normal and the bulk of their diet comes from corn, beans, squash, rice and various teas, soups and stews. The author thought that the calcium intake of mothers was low and that their diet was also low in protein, ascorbic acid and vitamin B, although detailed research on diet did not appear to have been carried out.

This study found interesting information concerning how 'modern' ideas about nutrition for pregnant and breastfeeding women had been grafted on to these indigenous beliefs. Mothers had heard about vitamins and orange juice through occasional contacts with health professionals. For most mothers vitamins were thought to be built into the constituents of some foods that imparted vigour to the foods they inhabited. Nevertheless they were thought to be inappropriate for pregnant women and babies as they were too 'strong' for infants and too 'fattening' for pregnant women. By and large it was thought that 'heavy' foods contained the most vitamins. Orange juice had been vigorously endorsed by health workers and the medical profession in Peru and was regarded by villagers as a desirable supplement for adults, especially if they were sick, and for children of school age. Orange juice was not, however, considered suitable for a baby consuming only milk as the baby's body would not be prepared for such a food and the combination could be bad for the infant's digestion. Generally the baby's digestion was prepared for accepting food other than milk by giving the child certain fruit when it was thought that the child's body was sufficiently developed to deal with it. This was part of the wider idea that the child needed to be prepared at each stage of its growth for the ingestion of different sorts of food and no child was given orange juice until it had been given fruit. The drink was therefore not considered acceptable to young babies and small children.

Mothers in Mexico (Millard and Graham, 1984) also structure their diet during breastfeeding according to certain hot/cold theories. Foods to encourage breast milk production include 'pulque' which is a fermented juice of the 'maguey' plant. The author thought that this probably did help breastfeeding mothers as it contained ethanol which could help with the 'let down' reflex, as well as giving extra nourishment to the mother. Another food which is thought to promote the production of breast milk is 'ajonjolin' which is a paste made from sesame seeds which, as the author points out, increases the mother's intake of calcium and phosphorus.

Among tribal groups in Andrah Pradesh in India (Vimala and Ratnaprabbha, 1987), one way of increasing the mother's supply of breast milk is to grind up an earthworm into a smooth paste, mix it with dall and give it to the mother without her knowledge. Another way is to make the mother swallow a live, small fish. The authors of this article list a number of different foods which mothers either ate more of or excluded from their diets during the period of breastfeeding. Despite this the authors described these mothers as not taking special care of themselves while breastfeeding. It was true that they did not eat in the same way as they might have been expected to by biomedically oriented doctors, but within the parameters of what they believed to be healthy and unhealthy food they took very good care indeed.

Ideas about how breast milk is produced may also influence what is considered to be the correct diet to produce plenty of it. For instance in Mithila (Reissland and Burghart, 1988), there are several ideas concerning how breast milk is produced in the body rather than one overall explanation. Each theme has an explanatory value in a particular context which gives rise to different ideas as to which is the most suitable food to encourage the production of breast milk. The first theme is that the human breast is an organ that converts water into milk. This theme stems from the observation that the breasts begin to swell in the sixth month of pregnancy and are said to do so with 'water' which refers not only to water but also to other bodily fluids. A mother's 'real' milk is not ready at the time of her child's birth but comes two or three days later when the heat in her body transforms this water into milk. This is one reason for eating 'halwa', a powerful heating tonic, 12 hours after giving birth. Milk at the top of the breast is considered thin, while that at the bottom is thick, rich, heavy and possibly difficult for the baby to digest. For this reason breasts need to be massaged with a circular massage prior to breastfeeding so that the milk is of an even consistency.

The second explanation is like the first but blood is substituted for water and this theory figures largely in explanations as to why a woman cannot produce good milk. Blood pervades the body and as it enters the breasts it is turned into milk. During pregnancy the child is nourished in the mother's womb by her blood and after birth receives nourishment from her breasts. Since nourishment comes from the same substance once the child is born, the mother's blood turns into milk in order that the child can be adequately fed. These theories suggest that the body is a system of transformation in which water or blood is converted into milk. The third explanation implies that no transformation takes place but that breast milk is in the breasts from the time of puberty. When the breasts swell during pregnancy it simply means that there is more milk there than before. The advice given to breastfeeding mothers is therefore to drink more milk which goes straight to her breasts and becomes breast milk. This theory gives further support for the idea that colostrum is curdled milk, because it is in the breast during pregnancy when the baby is not there to drink it so that it becomes stale.

Much of the research on this subject has focused on finding out what mothers say they should eat rather than what they actually do eat. Like the taboos associated with pregnancy, however, a mother can take a very idiosyncratic view of such ideas and will be expected to adapt them according to the nature of herself and her baby. For many women, and I have met many of them on my travels, there is no choice. As an Indian breastfeeding mother once told me,

> 'Yes there are special things I should eat but we can't afford to have special food in this village.'

The problem for her, as with so many women in less developed countries, is in getting enough food to eat, rather than special food. Often there are cultural practices which mean that women are less well nourished than men. Although women are generally responsible for preparing food and in some cases growing it as well, they may have little control over what is bought and they may not be able to eat until everyone else has eaten. Although women may have special food in the days immediately following birth, many women nurture their babies, and are expected to do so, at the expense of their own health.

CHAPTER FOUR

The Question of Colostrum

Colostrum is the fluid from the mother's breast which is available to the newborn during the first few days of life. It is a complex and ever-changing substance which affects the newborn in various positive ways and has many properties which are especially adapted for the optimum nutritional needs of the human baby. In the beginning (Odent, 1992; Stuart-Macadam, 1995), just after birth, colostrum stimulates peristaltic action in the digestive system. This acts like a purge or laxative which helps to eliminate the meconium which is the dark green, sticky substance in the gastrointestinal tracts of babies at birth. Colostrum also contains a concentration of many antibodies, the most copious of which is called IgA. This cannot be made by the newborn or be received through the placenta, yet it is necessary to protect the fragile mucous membranes of the bowels and respiratory tract. Fortunately it is available in colostrum during the first hours after birth in tens of milligrams per millilitre to carry out this function. During the time that colostrum is available, its qualities change in unique ways. A protective interlocking system against disease is available through the breastfeeding contact between mother and baby, to provide a defence against the specific germs and diseases to which a particular newborn is exposed. A mother's body manufactures protective antibodies to the germs in the environment which she shares with her baby and these are passed to the baby in the colostrum. Thus colostrum not only protects the baby from troublesome bacteria in the new environment outside the womb, but also stimulates the baby's own immune system which will not grow to maturity for a few months. Its protective properties make it the ideal food for the newborn.

In many traditional communities, however, these positive characteristics are not recognized, and even in the west, it is only relatively recently that these benefits have been known and acknowledged. Until the end of the 17th century in Europe (Fildes, 1986), mothers were advised not to breastfeed their newborns for up to a month after birth. It was thought that if the newborn drank colostrum while still passing meconium, this and the colostrum would coagulate in the intestines and cause problems. This was related to the idea that the mother's first milk or 'beestings' was unpurified because of her own impurity which extended from birth to the time until the lochia had stopped flowing and she had been 'churched'. It was also felt that until this time the mother was not rested enough to breastfeed. During this period the baby would be fed by another breastfeeding woman and the first milk would be drawn off either by a puppy, sucking glasses or an older child and discarded.

The protective effects of colostrum were first shown in a very practical way through the experiments of an English doctor called William Hunter in the 1750s. His aim was to reduce the morbidity and mortality from milk fever, which at that time was feared almost as much as the puerperal fever that caused many deaths. In the experiments he carried out in the Lying-in Hospital in Brownlow Street he showed that mothers who gave their babies colostrum were much less likely to contract milk fever. He therefore encouraged the (mainly poor) mothers at this hospital to give their babies colostrum with very positive results. There is a suggestion that as these changes in neonatal feeding practices became gradually more general they may have had a positive effect on infant mortality, although this is difficult to prove definitively.

Until relatively recently, however, midwives and other health professionals put no real emphasis on making sure that babies received colostrum. In a midwifery book by Johnstone published in 1926, for example, midwives are advised to make sure the child is put to the breast only three or four times on the first day after birth. This is mainly to encourage the newborn to learn to suck, although it is also mentioned that colostrum is a beneficial laxative. A similar textbook published in 1932 suggests a similar regime for similar reasons, but adding that there is little colostrum in the breasts and that if the baby is allowed to suck too much on an empty breast this can have disastrous effects. It will provoke sore nipples and make the baby dissatisfied with sucking. Then when the milk does come in the baby will not be interested in sucking it properly. Even a textbook by Gibberd, published in 1951, says that, although colostrum does have some anti-infective elements, the mother should breastfeed only for very short periods of a few minutes in the days immediately after birth. This book describes colostrum as being 'of little value as food', the suckling of it being merely a 'useful training for mother and child'. All these books suggest giving the baby boiled water during the first few days of life to make sure that the baby does not become dehydrated. Only when the milk comes in, on or after the third day, should breastfeeding begin in earnest and the baby be allowed to suck for 10–15 minutes at each feed.

Throughout the world there are many communities which consider that colostrum is not a good food for the newborn, although there may be no real explanation for this and mothers may disagree about whether it should be given or not. In Yemen (Beckerleg, 1991), for instance, less than half the new mothers surveyed started breastfeeding from the first day of birth, most waiting until the third day when the milk came in. Known as 'the yellow' in many parts of Yemen, mothers vehemently disagreed about whether it should be given to newborns or not. Maybe mothers connected this substance with the idea that the mother's body was polluted just after birth. Withholding colostrum was a way of distancing the baby from the mother and not feeding the baby something which came from a polluted place.

In Mexico (Skeel and Good, 1988; Millard and Graham, 1984), colostrum is thought to be bad for the baby because it has been in the breast for some time and is therefore old milk. At the same time it is thought that if the mother produces colostrum during the pregnancy she will later have good supplies of breast milk. In Guatemala, colostrum is not considered fit for consumption and in Peru colostrum is thought of as waste rather like the meconium. It is believed to block the milk flow, foul the child's stomach and perhaps be fatal for the newborn. Mothers therefore squeeze out and dispose of colostrum as they do the wastes of childbirth and menstruation – by burial.

In a study carried out in Indonesia (Hull, Thapa and Pratomo, 1990) only a third (38 per cent) of the mothers interviewed recognized the importance of colostrum and many felt that the 'yellow milk' would upset the baby's stomach. Older women with more children and those with less education – and presumably with more traditional ideas – were more likely to feel that this was so. The main reason given for its dislike was its 'dirty' yellow appearance. In the Philippines (Fernandez and Guthrie, 1984), among a sample of mothers living in the squatter areas of a Philippine city, most offered their baby the breast immediately after birth. The majority of mothers made sure the baby was fed colostrum but this was not so throughout the Philippines. Those who expressed and discarded colostrum did so because it did not have the colour and texture of milk and because they felt it had been in the breast too long.

Traditional ideas about colostrum in Africa vary between different groups. In Mali (Dettwyler, 1995), for instance, colostrum is called 'dark breast water' and is considered neither good nor bad for the baby, merely 'what is in the breasts before the milk comes'. Amongst the Pedi (Chalmers, 1990), in South Africa, although a third of the sample said that colostrum was good for the baby, a large majority (81.7 per cent) thought that water was better and nearly half (46.3 per cent) that formula was better still. Urban mothers were more likely to say that colostrum was good for the baby than rural mothers, perhaps reflecting their greater exposure to western medical ideas.

Given the known benefits of colostrum it has to be asked why historically for so long and now in so many traditional societies, mothers do not feed their babies this valuable substance. This is especially relevant in places where pre-lacteal feeds are likely to be contaminated and an infective risk to the baby. Little research has been carried out on this particular subject, particularly that which explores the subjective perceptions about colostrum and why it should not be given. That is, of course, if the mother has an explanation for why she does not feed the newborn colostrum as, in my experience in India, many mothers do not do so because 'we just don't'. One piece of research which does throw some light on this issue is a study carried out in Guinea Bissau, Africa (Gunnlaugsson and Einarsdottir, 1993). Detailed information was obtained from 20 respected, elderly women from different ethnic groups, living as subsistence farmers, who were perceived by their communities to be knowledgeable about traditional aspects of birth. Of great interest was the fact that these women came from different cultural groups, some of which avoided colostrum and some of which did not.

All respondents noticed there was a difference in consistency and colour between colostrum and breast milk which was generally described as unpleasant, watery looking and of red/yellow colour. The taste was considered bad and irritating for the baby but opinions differed on its quality. The Balanta tribal group thought colostrum unsuitable for the newborn and that breastfeeding should therefore be delayed for three to four days until the 'real milk' came in. They described colostrum as dirty, insufficient (as a food for the baby), the cause of many diseases and in some cases the death of an infant. They thought colostrum should therefore be discarded and pre-lacteal feeds, consisting of undiluted cow's milk or sugared water, be given instead. One of the explanations for this practice was that in their mythology the Tribal Father had survived thanks to the cow's milk he received after his mother had died at birth. The Balanta like to pay respect to this before starting breastfeeding by performing a ritual at the

Tribal Father's sacred place. Since this was some distance away it could delay breastfeeding for up to a week.

The Papel, Manjaco and Mancanha groups also thought that colostrum was an insufficient food as it had no nutritional value. Unlike the Balanta, however, they did not feel that it was actively harmful apart from occasionally causing diarrhoea. The mother could therefore start breastfeeding immediately after birth. A woman from the Bijago said that she thought colostrum was concentrated. For this reason it might cause diarrhoea but this cleaned the stomach, did no harm and never killed. In those groups, where there was a gap between birth and breastfeeding because the colostrum was considered inadequate, a wet nurse was preferable. This allowed the mother to throw away her colostrum and start breastfeeding when the mature milk came in. Otherwise pre-lacteal feeds were given.

Informants from Islamic groups had generally positive ideas about breast milk. The Fula and Mandinga informants considered it best to start breastfeeding 6–12 hours after birth but thought there was no harm in starting right away. According to the Fula, colostrum gave babies strength and protection against diseases, but it could be bad from a woman who was primiparous or had very dark areolas. If the colostrum of a particular woman was judged bad then it could irritate the mouth of child and/or cause diarrhoea in which case a wet nurse was recruited. The Beafada claimed that all breast milk was good, but preferred to give a herbal mixture to the newborn while waiting for the milk to come in. All these different groups had a special name for colostrum and the Mandinga had different names for the breast milk at different stages of the baby's development, e.g. first week, first month, until the child can walk and after learning to walk.

Whatever the ideas about colostrum it was usually some hours after birth before breastfeeding was initiated, and starting to breastfeed immediately after birth was not the rule amongst these rural women. The authors point out that the idea of breastfeeding starting immediately after birth seems new, even in the west, and has been brought about as the result of medical research. Although by modern standards breastfeeding started late in these groups, in the majority of cases there was a far more prolonged lactation than in the west.

The authors questioned why colostrum was so widely disliked amongst these women and whether there was an explanation for why it was or was not given. Looking at how colostrum was perceived by mothers it seemed that colour and consistency were a contributing factor and that maybe they also associated it with meconium. Mothers also felt that because it was secreted during the last weeks of pregnancy, it seemed old and stale and therefore not suitable for the newborn. It was hypothesized that not giving colostrum to the newborn may have been a reaction to high infant mortality. Not giving colostrum immediately after birth ensured that mothers did not form too close a tie to the neonate thus minimizing the emotional trauma should the baby die. This explanation did not hold, however, as high infant mortality was found in all groups, whether or not colostrum was given to their babies. Thus the reason for this behaviour which appeared to deny the newborn the best possible start in life remained a puzzle.

In India colostrum is generally perceived to be bad for the newborn, although this is changing amongst more educated mothers who may have been more exposed to western medical ideas. In one study (Katiyar et al., 1981), for example, it was found that 90 per cent of poor mothers from an urban slum and a rural area believed that colostrum was harmful, while only 63 per cent of those from a higher socio-economic group (and therefore probably with more education) believed this to be so. In another study (Chandrashekar, 1985), three-quarters of the sample believed that colostrum should be fed to babies with the numbers believing this increasing with increased education.

The study from Mithila, in the north of India, however, found that the desire not to give colostrum was related to a number of indigenous views about the wider context in which birth took place. These concerned the nature of the baby and mother immediately after birth and also local ideas concerning digestion and what foods are and are not easily digested. Mothers were unanimous in their feeling that colostrum was not a good food and should not be fed to the newborn. One explanation was that as the blood of birth was foul so was the colostrum which had been in the mother's body during the pregnancy. It was believed that a baby who drank colostrum would vomit. Other women said that colostrum was not milk but rather pus that oozed from the body. The researchers questioned this attitude given that everyone in the community was quite happy to drink the first milk of a cow or buffalo. Local women pointed out, however, that this was always cooked before eating and as a result the milk separated into curds and whey showing that it was milk that had soured. Despite the tenacity of this belief about the negative qualities of colostrum, it was probable that some babies did get some colostrum as all the women they observed started breastfeeding within 24 hours of birth. Colostrum was expressed not on the first but the second day after birth just prior to breastfeeding.

Fundamental to this belief was that on the day of giving birth the mother was neither in a state to feed or be fed. After completion of labour, mothers were given warm milk to drink and then 12 hours later a tonic of 'halwa'. It was thought that the exertion of labour and birth disturbed the process of digestion and the mother could not digest solid food until her stomach/womb had recovered from giving birth. Her first proper meal was not consumed until the second day. During this time the baby was looked after by others who fussed over it and either gave it to a wet nurse or fed it warm cow's milk. At this stage the mother was not expected to establish an exclusive relationship with the baby as she was thought to be too exhausted from the physical work of labour to do so. It was pointed out that the prohibition of feeding what was considered stale milk to the neonate formed part of a pattern of minimal tentative contact between mother and child immediately postpartum. The researchers felt that the taboo against colostrum had been isolated from its cultural context and this was why it had been misunderstood by the biomedical establishment. They had focused only on the fact of the withholding of colostrum, not seeing it as only one aspect of a total cultural environment.

In India the Ayurvedic (traditional Indian) system of medicine has an explanation of why colostrum should not be given to the newborn, elements of which were apparent in the research carried out in Mithila. Ayurveda (Heyn, 1987 and Lad Vasant, 1993) is a system of medicine that is still widely practised in India and, like many indigenous systems, encompasses not only the physical but the psychological and spiritual aspects of life of both of the individual and universe. While every individual is unique, he or she is at the same time a part of a wider existence, being composed of the same energies and matter which follow the same laws.

In Ayurveda all existence is derived from the union of Spirit and Matter which come together to form 'Mahat' or the Cosmic Intelligence which is both in the universe and a part of which is within each individual. All matter is composed of five elements. Living matter, however, in addition to these elements also has within itself the three forces which regulate all the biological processes. These are called 'vata' (air), which is responsible for all the body's sensations; 'pitta' (fire), responsible for anything where heat is generated and in particular the transformation of food to energy and 'kapha' (water and earth) which is responsible for the body's structure.

The human body is perceived as being composed of innumerable channels which maintain the metabolism of the various tissues and govern the process of assimilation and elimination. The health of the body is determined by the functioning of 'agni,' the biological fire which governs the metabolism. When agni is good, food is digested properly and all the channels of the body work well. When it is poor, the channels become blocked and the three basic energies become out of balance which leads to ill-health. In Ayurveda treatment is not, therefore, symptomatic but goes to the root of the person's physical and psychological being and brings the person to his or her natural self harmony and thus harmony with the universe. In India the explanation as to why the newborn should not be given colostrum therefore has to be viewed in the light of these Ayurvedic principles.

In Ayurvedic medicine (Vasudevsastri, 1990; Muralidhar and Madhuri, 1990), milk is in general considered to be a very wholesome food that gives good nourishment throughout one's life. It strengthens the body and intellect and acts as a tonic. Only in certain debilitating conditions is milk to be avoided. According to Ayurvedic principles, the newborn baby is in something of a debilitated state. Just after birth there is a predominance of kapha in the newborn's body which keeps the digestive fire or pitta in a subdued state. This means that if the baby is breastfed immediately after birth, it will aggravate the kapha within the body leading to more congestion of energies and disharmony of energies which will weaken the baby still further. Before the baby is breastfed the body should be decongested by giving the baby a mixture of honey, clarified butter and gold. This cleansing will clear the passages, thus stimulating the pitta fire and digestion and giving the baby more strength so that the baby's system can digest milk more easily.

At birth the breasts of the mother are congested. Owing to this congestion the milk (colostrum) in her breasts stagnates, which in turn makes it 'guru' or hard to digest, which increases its density. Although colostrum resembles milk, it is not milk, but is dense and promotes kapha. If it is given to the newborn it intensifies the already debilitated state of the baby. It increases 'phlegm' (which is a kind of 'heavy' energy rather than actual phlegm) and digestive problems still further thus weakening the baby even more. According to Ayurvedic principles, colostrum is not a good food for the newborn, not because of its purely physical qualities but because of its stagnant energies and how these intensify the already debilitated energies within the baby. For this reason the baby should not be fed until three days after birth when the pure milk of the mother has come in. According to this view the best way for a mother to ensure the optimum health of her baby and herself is to feed the newborn the things which will cure the initial debilitation, such as the mixture previously described. She should then take the necessary action to clear the stagnant colostrum from her breasts which will enable the pure breast milk to flow well, thereby enabling her to successfully breastfeed her baby. When a mother breastfeeds her baby, this has both social and spiritual significance as well as nourishing the baby physically.

Looked at from a purely physical point of view, it would seem that in many traditional communities the health of many newborns are compromised because they do not receive colostrum and all its valuable benefits. Even from this brief survey it is obvious that there are many conscious reasons for this ranging from its colour, ideas about the purity of the mother after birth or as part of a complex system of a traditional medical practice such as Ayurveda. Are there deeper reasons? Michel Odent thinks there are and believes that it stems from a desire on the part of society to disturb the initial mother–child relationship and thus develop a certain kind of individual of use to an aggressive and warlike society. From the beginning of human evolution, he says, the most successful human groups are those which have had the capacity to destroy other groups. The most efficient way of making a group of humans into super predators is to disturb the mother–newborn relationship so that from the very beginning the newborn loses a certain trust in others and develops an insensitivity towards them. He thinks that withholding colostrum is part of a series of things (which include neonatal circumcision, swaddling and baptism in cold water) which all have the same meaning and end, which is to disturb the newborn's relationship with the mother. Evidence for this point of view is available, he says, from those civilizations which have been able to survive without having to destroy others. Usually they are integrated more thoroughly with the ecosystem and often isolated in inhospitable terrain which provides them with protection. Such communities find it unnecessary to disturb the relationship between mother and newborn and tend to feed their babies colostrum.

While this is an interesting theory much more empirical information is needed for its justification. More research needs to be done on this subject cross-culturally to determine whether there are differences between those communities which withhold colostrum and those which do not. In the already mentioned research from Guinea-Bissau, for example, there were very different ideas about the value of colostrum among cultural groups from apparently similar geographical backgrounds. Clearly there were many factors of relevance and the researchers themselves were unable to come up with a coherent explanation. Building up a picture of the events at birth which have relevance later in life is also difficult and complex. Opinion is divided on the extent to which things that happen before and around birth cause particular psychological and physical effects in later life. Again it is likely that there are a pattern of influences of which the withholding or not of colostrum is likely to be only one aspect.

Michel Odent goes on to say that in the current age of ecological consciousness the priority to dominate other groups and destroying life is no longer relevant. A more holistic view is necessary and this, he implies, will automatically lead to mothers giving their babies colostrum. It seems to me, however, that a more integrated world view concerning the place of humans within the universe does not necessarily lead to this outcome. As has already been mentioned, the Ayurvedic view, while taking a very holistic view of the person within the universe, considers that colostrum should not be given to the newborn. In fact, according to the Ayurvedic view, a mother will do better not to give her baby colostrum because it will prepare both her and the baby for later successful breastfeeding on a long-term basis. Even in the light of the proven beneficial physical properties of colostrum, many Ayurvedic doctors do not think this is sufficient justification to allow babies to have it. For them it is not just the physical characteristics of colostrum which are important, but also the other energies viewed in a holistic way – and who is to say which is correct when the two medical systems work in such very different ways?

This question is of considerable importance when it comes to government or WHO efforts to encourage mothers to give their babies colostrum. Often this encouragement is made in direct contradiction to traditional ideas about the negative effects that colostrum can have on newborns. The problem with this (as explained by the authors of the research in Guinea-Bissau) is that such encouragement tends to be presented as a set of rules or guidelines that mothers have to follow in order to breastfeed successfully. Thus one set of guidelines based on traditional ideas is substituted for another set based on biomedicine. If mothers may find themselves unable to accept either set of rules or guidelines completely – maybe after giving birth in hospital and then returning to their family – then feelings of confusion and inadequacy may result. Mothers may respond by turning to bottle feeding, if they can afford it, which is not subject to all these restrictions and which is much less emotionally charged. Thus encouraging mothers to give their babies colostrum may, if done insensitively, actually lead to less breastfeeding.

To me, the questions raised by this extremely brief look at the way colostrum is traditionally viewed shows that this is a subject which merits further investigation, which is beyond the scope of this short chapter. Unlike traditions of birth, which, in many cases seem to support the physical process, traditions concerning colostrum seem to do the opposite. The health of many newborns are put at more risk because they are not given this valuable substance. At the same time, within certain indigenous medical systems, such as Ayurveda and in Mexico, women feel they are doing the best for themselves and their babies by not giving colostrum. It seems to me that the questions this raises are crucial to a deeper understanding of ourselves both as physical beings and as part of a wider social and universal environment.

CHAPTER FIVE

What's in Mother's Milk?

As I watched my baby grow, nurtured by the milk of my body, it seemed to me like a miracle. I did not know what was in my milk, but seeing how my baby thrived, it seemed like the perfect gift. Later, in a more academic frame of mind, I found out something about what was in my milk. How breast milk has the right balance of protein, carbohydrates and sugar for the baby's growth as well as other substances which help against infection and which cannot be manufactured in a formula. How it contains species-specific concentrations of hormones and other bioactive compounds. How these may be responsible for optimum development of the baby's gastrointestinal tract, pituitary gland, pancreas and brain. Breast milk is a living substance, and as such we still don't know everything about all its constituents and the changes that it goes through, in order to nurture the babies who live on it. Something of the miracle nature of this substance is also there in traditional ideas about breast milk. These often go far beyond its physical characteristics and physical nurturing qualities as defined by western ideas of biomedicine.

The quality of a mother's milk is perceived as being totally in balance with the particular needs of her baby amongst the Amele, a group in Papua New Guinea (Jenkins, Orr-Ewing and Heywood, 1984). The physical quality of breast milk is thought to change from a watery weak fluid, when the baby is born, to a stronger one as lactation proceeds. This is in accordance with the development of the child and its need for more nutrition as it grows. The mother is perceived as producing breast milk which is of exactly the right 'strength' for the developmental needs of her baby. If 'strong' breast milk intended for an older child is given to a younger child, it is thought to cause constipation and/or a swollen belly. Wet nursing is not, therefore, perceived as an option in this community as milk appropriate for the mother's baby will, in all probability, not be correct for any other baby. Since colostrum looks more watery than mature milk, older women consider it a good food for the newborn, although at the time this study was undertaken, young mothers were discarding it thinking that its colour made it a noxious substance.

In Mathila (Reissland and Burghart, 1988), health and longevity are believed to be the natural outcome of a proper diet, this being perceived in terms of the indigenous Ayurvedic system of medicine rather than the western biomedical one. Applied to babies or toddlers it follows that health or illness stems from the quality of the mother's milk. If a baby becomes ill, this is explained in terms of there being some harmful quality in the mother which has been transferred to the baby through the milk. Another theory is that a mother may be 'weak' so that the breast milk she produces is thin or insufficient. Worst of all is when a mother's milk diminishes in quantity and stops altogether. In this case the milk of a cow or buffalo might be used but this is considered a very poor substitute and it will probably be diluted with water. A wet nurse will probably not be considered a good option as she might transfer illness from herself to the child. In such cases when a child is fed an alternative to the mother's milk, but remains sickly, it is still the mother's fault, even though the milk is not personally hers. Whatever the physical or other reason for her lack of milk, the question of medical causation cannot be separated from the issue of personal responsibility on the part of the mother.

Interesting ideas about the qualities of breast milk compared to formula are found amongst mothers in Mali (Dettwyler, 1987). It is generally believed that breast milk is the best food for babies as not only does it make the baby strong and healthy, it also makes the baby 'heavy'. Bottle-fed infants are perceived as being weaker and some say that although formula can make a child grow tall, it will not be so 'heavy' or healthy and strong. Several women said that breast milk protected against disease and that breast milk was an important nourishment for babies when they were ill. Several women claimed that infants were stronger 'in the old days' when it was more usual for them to be breastfed up to the age of three or four.

Despite these perceived positive qualities of breast milk, it is also thought to vary both in quantity and quality between different women, this being judged by the health and size of the baby. The mother of a fat baby obviously has 'good' milk while that of a thin baby has 'bad' milk. The quality of breast milk is something intrinsic to a woman and not much can be done about it if it is perceived as being inadequate. This ties up with ideas about how breast milk is produced in the body. It is thought to be made 'from the blood' and that each person has a finite amount of blood for their lifetime and it is impossible to make up for any loss of blood which is gone due to illness or accident. Older women who have nursed many children are thought not to make much breast milk, having used up all their blood in the conversion to breast milk for previous babies. Once breast milk has been produced and is in the breasts, it should be used quickly otherwise it is likely to turn bad. If a child consumes such 'old' milk it could give the child diarrhoea and cause vomiting. In this situation the milk becomes 'hot' and the child should not be allowed to drink it as he or she will become sick. Menstrual blood is also perceived as 'hot' in a similar way and can affect breast milk by making it 'hot' so that the child gets a fever. Since a child should not be fed 'stale breast milk' it is thought that weaning should be quick. Once a child has stopped breastfeeding, they should not restart as they would be drinking old and stale breast milk which could make them ill.

Children are thought to be related to their father through his semen and to their mother via her breast milk. If a woman breastfeeds the baby of another woman she is passing, through her milk, the same relationship that she has with her biological children to that baby. Thus all the children that a woman breastfeeds are considered to be related through the milk of the mother and as 'milk relatives' are not allowed to marry.

Similar ideas are found in Bangladesh (Blanchet, 1991) where breast milk is thought to be like 'blood' in terms of it being a shared vital substance. The idea of 'blood' is central to the idea of what makes a lineage but in this patrilineal society, men and women's blood is considered very different. A man's blood (and this includes semen which is thought of as concentrated blood) has an inherited coded substance which the father passes to his child at conception. Both boys and girls receive their father's blood, but only boys are able to pass on the inherited coded substance that it contains. Women's blood, and this includes their breast milk, is perceived as a nurturing substance essential to life and growth but it is not a coded substance and cannot therefore establish a lineage. Women are perceived as receptacles, often associated with the earth, which takes the seed in its womb. Men must choose 'good' pure women to carry the children of their lineage, as some of the mother's physical and moral qualities are said to pass to her children through her 'blood' or breast milk. It is also thought important that the vital substances of mother and father, which together make the child, are compatible. For Hindus these are codified in the caste system and its associated marriage rules. For Muslims the rules are less elaborate, but it is important that women are pure receptacles for the men's seed and that men and women's vital substances meet only in marriage. Women who have gone through a number of marital unions, even though legal in Islam, are regarded as progressively defiled and spoiled and therefore less pure.

Breast milk has powerful inherent properties, but in many communities it is thought that a mother's physical and emotional state can negatively affect the milk, which will be passed on to the baby with bad effects. This means that a mother must constantly be aware of what she is doing and how this might affect her breast milk. In Mexico (Skeel and Good, 1988), for instance, eating or drinking while breastfeeding may render the milk bad for the baby, as will getting angry or frightened. In the Philippines (Fernandez and Guthrie, 1984) it is thought that if a mother stays too long in the sun, the milk becomes stale. If this happens, mothers are advised to express the milk and discard it and then wait for a little time left before feeding the baby again. Similarly, milk should not stay in the breast for more than six hours, and if this happens it should be expressed and discarded in the same way. The consequences for the baby of carrying on breastfeeding in such a situation could be weakness and susceptibility to a range of illnesses. To ward off such consequences mothers sometimes express a few drops of milk on to the baby's fontanelle and put the sign of the cross on the baby's head, navel and extremities to bar the passage of air from the mother to the infant's body. It is also thought that the mood of the mother, especially negative states like anger or grief, can be transmitted to the child by way of the breast milk. When this happens, especially if the mother is in a long-term stressful situation such as a broken marriage, it is a reason to stop breastfeeding either for a time or even permanently. A Philippino mother in an unhappy marriage was once heard to say that she was not going to breastfeed as she did not want her baby to 'suck up her sorrow'.

Fear, anger, sickness or sun can all turn the mother's milk 'bad' in a similar way in the Yemen (Beckerleg, 1991). In general mothers feel that breast milk is good but that for specific reasons her own milk can very easily turn bad. Breastfeeding has possible dangers and to do so successfully is an almost superhuman task. Mothers seldom mention their capacity to pass on positive qualities to their children, but tend to focus on the possible negative things that they can transmit. Mothers should not become angry, sick or afraid and must be careful of the sun. Everyday domestic duties create further worries. Heat from the bread baking oven can be harmful and the hot work of baking bread can 'make the milk like water'. If breast milk happens to fall on the oven this can 'dry the milk up'. The local word for bread also means 'life' and it seems that nurturing life by baking bread and nurturing life by breastfeeding are often incompatible. Other women are also a danger, as envy from them in the form of the 'evil eye' can make it difficult for a woman to breastfeed. Protective charms used to avoid this include quotes from the Koran, painting kohl around the eyes of the child and using the herb rue. If a child becomes sick this can be because of bad milk and often as a result a mother will stop breastfeeding.

Breast milk is considered by the Khmir in northern Tunisia (Dreyghton, 1992) to be a very powerful substance which is part of the life sustaining force or 'baraka'. When a mother breastfeeds a thriving baby this shows that the life sustaining force is flowing, not only from mother to baby but throughout the household as well. As in Yemen, however, Khmir mothers think that their milk can become bad if the baby is given breast milk too soon after the mother has been doing heavy physical work, like fetching wood from the mountain. As the mother's body becomes overheated from doing such work, the milk clots and becomes indigestible, although it is thought to return to its usual state half an hour after the body returns to its normal temperature. Other physical transformations to the breast milk can take place if the woman eats earth (a common remedy for anaemia in this community), grain from the new harvest or buttermilk from a cow that has recently calved. A breastfeeding mother, therefore, has to take care about what she does, as any inadequacy on her part can lead to the baby developing 'milk illness'. At the same time, however, a mother might break any or all of these restrictions if she feels overwhelmed by her baby's need to be fed. Her explanation of how she could not wait to feed the baby on hearing him or her cry is seen as evidence of her tender maternal feelings, so that she is not necessarily to blame. The cure for 'milk illness' is to carry out a ritual for the baby, the elements of which focus on healing the mother–baby relationship. It provides the mother with a strong positive self-image in her ability to transmit life, vitality and prosperity through her actions and particularly with her breastfeeding. After this ritual the baby accepts the breast and the symptoms of milk illness disappear. Once again the mother is capable of transmitting the supernatural essence necessary to the well-being of her family which gives her the right to her central place in the home.

Traditional tests and remedies for 'bad milk'

The best proof of the quality of a mother's milk is the steady, healthy growth of her baby. Where a baby fails to thrive, it is assumed that there must be something wrong with the mother's milk, but in our test ridden biomedicine, tests on the physical constituents of a mother's milk are very rarely carried out. The only test likely to be carried out, and perhaps less so now than in past years, is the test weighing of the baby after each feed to determine how much milk the baby has eaten, although this has to be carried out very carefully over a period of time if the results are to have any validity at all. There are, however, many traditional tests for breast milk quality which were used in historical times in the west and are still used in traditional communities today. Although often such tests were used to test the quality of breast milk in a proposed wet nurse, rather than for a mother, whose milk it is assumed will be of the right quality for her baby. There is considerable historical evidence as to the nature of the tests, but unfortunately there is little evidence to show how often they were used or the efficacy of the cures should the test show that the milk was not good. Traditional ways of improving breast milk quality, should it be necessary, include harnessing spiritual forces as well as making physical and emotional changes.

In ancient Rome there were several methods for testing the consistency of the milk, the best known being 'the nail test' often credited to Soranus, although it was also described by Pliny a century earlier. This was used for several centuries and was still being quoted in midwifery books of the 17th century in Europe (Fildes, 1986).

> 'Moderately thick milk will be recognized by the fact that if a drop is made to fall on the fingernail or a leaf of sweet bay or on something else of equal smoothness, it spreads gently and when rocked it retains... the same form. Milk which runs off immediately is watery, whereas milk that stays together like honey and remains motionless is thick.'

Another widely described test was to mix breast milk with twice its amount of water. Ideally it should stay the same for a short while and then dissolve and remain white in colour:

> 'For milk which dissolves immediately is watery, and it is worse if it is reduced into fibrous streaks like water in which meat has been washed, for such milk is also raw. But milk which does not disperse for some length of time and settles, so that when the water is poured off it is found as a caseous substance all around the bottom, is thick and hard to digest.'

Soranus thought that the milk should be tested at different times since it could change its consistency under different conditions. He also pointed out that if a child was failing to thrive, it did not follow that the milk was inadequate but that maybe the child was being prevented by disease from getting the proper nourishment.

In ancient Egypt,

> 'To recognize milk which is bad: thou shalt perceive that its smell is like snj of fish. To recognize milk which is good: its smell is like powdered manna ...'

and in Byzantium,

> 'Pour an eighth part of the milk into a glass vessel; add rennet in proportion and stir with the fingers, then leave to set and see whether the curd is less than the whey, for such milk is no good, and the reverse is indigestible: the best is that which contains the both in equal proportions.'

The hair test was also very popular and also mentioned in later European midwifery books. Milk could be tested by using a hair moistened with milk and suspended in the air. If all the milk ran off, or if only a small drop stayed on one part, then this milk must be discarded. If milk clung to the entire hair then this was the best.

Other tests include one from China where 'a milk drop on the table should be round and raised and it should not be possible to blow it into smaller drops'. In Fiji, milk is put on a saucer and if flies settle on it, then it is poison milk.

In India, within the Ayurvedic system of medicine, the qualities of pure breast milk include the following:

- that it is cool to the touch;
- that it is the colour of conch (a shell) and free from impurities;
- that the taste is sweet, with a bitter subsidiary taste;
- that it is odourless;
- qualities which are life giving, light, promoting digestive fire, tonifying, strength giving, nutritive.

Being sweet and, at the same time, light is a distinctive quality of individual breast milk. An ancient test for the purity of milk was to put a drop of milk into a little water. It should, without floating or sinking, become one with the water. If no threads were present, then such milk was considered pure. From this viewpoint colostrum does not qualify for the meaning of pure milk as it will not dissolve in the water. Colostrum, according to this test, will be full of impurities, hard to digest and be debilitating for the newborn.

The research carried out in Guinea Bissau (Gunnlaugsson and Einarsdottir, 1993) found that under certain conditions mature milk, as well as colostrum, could be bad for the infant. Watching the development of the baby was important. If the baby was strong and healthy, the milk was good, whereas if the baby did not grow and was always sick with cough and diarrhoea then the milk was probably bad. This could be verified by looking at the colour and texture of the milk which was an important continuing quality control for most mothers. If it was yellow, red or had 'worms' (described as tiny little particles) the milk was probably bad. When the quality of the milk was in doubt, for whatever reason, the 'ant' test would be performed, this being used by all ethnic groups.

The mother expressed some milk into her hand or a calabash and put an ant into it. If the ant survived it showed the milk was good, whereas if it died the milk was bad. The treatment for this condition varied. The Fula had a ceremony in which the breasts were rubbed with red palm oil and then washed with a herbal mixture including peel of mango, culati and the bark of a blooming tree. During the ceremony breast milk already in the breast was discarded. If the ant test showed a positive result then breastfeeding would continue. Balanta mothers warmed their breasts with steam from a brew of a kind of honey, while Papel mothers warmed some sand in a cauldron, put it in a cotton cloth and rubbed their breasts with it. Beafada mothers boiled some special leaves in water, added red palm oil and washed their breasts with this liquid. Sometimes while having this treatment the mother would stop breastfeeding and a wet nurse would be recruited.

From the biomedical point of view, traditional ideas about 'bad milk' are usually perceived in a negative way as they often lead to, what western medical personnel consider, unnecessary cessation of breastfeeding or even in some cases a failure to start. This, of course, is one facet of the conflict between the biomedical way of looking at breastfeeding, which focuses on the physical process, and traditional concepts which take a more holistic view. When a mother is being urged by someone of the biomedical establishment to carry on breastfeeding when it runs counter to traditional ideas, this is a very conflicting situation for her. As one author has pointed out, if a mother disobeys traditional ideas at the expense of biomedical expertise and the baby continues to be sick or dies then she is in a very anomalous situation with regard to her family. She may well, in terms of family support, have more to lose by following biomedical expertise, especially if it fails to help the child.

Wet nursing

Most of the tests described above were of more importance to wet nurses than for mothers to find out about the quality of their own milk. In Europe from the 15th to the 18th century, wet nursing was a commercial activity of some importance. As Fildes points out, it was a way a woman could earn a reasonable amount of money for herself and yet has featured little in accounts of how women earned their living during this time. Wet nurses were used mostly by the aristocracy in Europe and there was considerable concern expressed in the medical literature about how best to choose a wet nurse.

Advice was given as to how to test for the quality of the milk which included the nail test described above together with smelling and tasting the milk, with quite detailed instructions being given as to the best way of doing this. Consistency was considered to be the most important criterion, with the milk not being too thick (considered unnatural and evil) or too thin (regarded as 'raw' and passing through the child too quickly). The nail test was still the most popular test to determine whether the quality of a certain breast milk was satisfactory. Another test suggested was to express some breast milk into a glass, add some rennet or myrrh, mix it and allow it to coagulate. The ideal breast milk had equal quantities of 'cheese' and 'whey'. If the solid were greater, it was too thick, while if the whey predominated it was too thin, and in both cases the person should be rejected as a wet nurse. The hair test was also suggested as was dropping milk into the eyes to see if it made them sting – another reason for rejection. Throughout most of the period the ideal colour of breast milk was thought to be white and anyone with milk coloured with blue, grey or yellow (probably indicative of a breast infection) should not be chosen. Later in the 18th century, probably as a result of more detailed and scientific observation of breast milk, that of a bluish or bluish white colour was also considered satisfactory. The milk should have a sweet and pleasant taste. If it was salty then it was unwholesome, if sour or bitter it would affect the baby's stomach in a bad way and any other strong or strange taste would mean that the milk was not suitable. Bad or infected breast milk could be detected by an unpleasant odour and would also be rejected, with the smell also telling something about the temperament of the woman.

Before 1800 the wet nurse or breastfeeding mother did not just provide nourishment for her baby but also transmitted all her ideas, beliefs, intelligence and diet, together with her other physical, mental and emotional qualities. The general character of the wet nurse, therefore, needed to be established, as well as the quality of the milk. This was generally done using the Greek humoral system, which was mentioned in medical texts until the end of the 17th century. Individuals were generally considered be of a certain 'disposition', these being indicated by one of four complexions:

1.   phlegmatic (cold and moist);
2.   melancholic (cold and dry);
3.   choleric (hot and dry); and,
4.   sanguine (hot and moist).

Children were believed to have varying degrees of hotness and moistness, which were sanguine characteristics, manifested by a ruddy complexion and light brown or chestnut hair. Thus wet nurses were preferred with these complexions which were also said to infer that the woman had better quality and quantity of milk, were disease free and without undesirable qualities. A few authors believed that the complexion of the wet nurse should be similar to the mother of the child and then the milk would agree with the baby better. The colour of the hair was thought to be the best indicator of the nurse's complexion so that extreme colours such as black, white or red were frowned upon. Red haired nurses with freckles were particularly dangerous as it was thought they had a bad, rank, strong smell and produced sour, stinking milk which caused thrush in the child and generally prejudiced the child's health. This feeling against red haired nurses originated in the ancient world and appears to have been particularly strong in France. By the 18th century British writers were questioning this idea.

It was also thought that the nurse should have milk of the right 'age', i.e. should have given birth to her own baby at about the same time so the milk was of the right 'strength'. Although this was mentioned in many texts it was also obvious that in practice many women continued to nurse a succession of babies as long as they had milk to do so. If a woman became pregnant or started menstruating, this could change the quality of the breast milk and make it unsuitable for the baby. Pregnancy led to less milk of poorer quality and menstruation did the same, as it was believed that breast milk was derived from the blood of menstruation. Wet nurses were therefore watched carefully to see they did not become pregnant or menstruate, both of which could lead to the termination of their employment. The wet nurse was seen as the cause of most infantile diseases and any treatment for the child was therefore given to her, since it would pass through the milk to the child.

Wet nursing has been reported in some traditional communities but probably more on an individual and less on a commercial basis than it was in Europe during the period described. This subject was discussed by the researchers in Mithila who were told that it was of great importance for a wet nurse to have the correct moral qualities. Babies were very prone to a contagious illness called 'saruva rog', which was a disease caused not only by physical contagion but also by negative impressions, registered by all modes of perception including through breast milk. When a wet nurse was needed, preference was given to a woman of good character, in practice a lactating female relative or a neighbour whom one respected as a sister. 'Big caste' families avoided recruiting wet nurses from amongst the untouchable or scheduled castes who were thought to have inferior mental, moral and physical qualities. Physical sickness transmitted by milk included chills and fevers to serious illnesses, such as TB and syphilis. It was thought that the breast milk of a wet nurse would need to be tested according to Ayurvedic principles to ensure that it did not contain disease provoking qualities.

Milk kinship

The power of breast milk to forge close ties between individuals on a family basis can be seen in the idea of milk kinship. In Mali and Yemen this power was apparent in that all children who had been breastfed by the same woman, whether they were biologically related or not, were considered to be related closely enough that marriage was not allowed between them. In Yemen, although breastfeeding the child of another woman was rarely undertaken, it was known that to do so created a kinship relationship where the wet nurse was considered as second mother. Her own children were considered siblings to the child she had nursed so that no marriage was possible between them.

The whole aspect of milk kinship has been explored by Jane Khatib-Chahidi (1992). She looks at the idea of milk kinship in Shi'ite Islamic Iran but describes various other places where it has also been found. The milk relationship comes into existence through a woman suckling another woman's child and no amount of rearing a child, for however long, can create the same relationship. Islamic Law defines three types of relationship: by blood, marriage and milk. All three involve an impediment to marriage between certain persons so related. The milk relationship is, however, legally restricted kinship as milk kin cannot inherit from each other, milk parents have no legal duty to maintain their milk children, nor do they have any form of guardianship over them. Although the milk mother fulfils the same practical purpose as the European wet nurse, there is a basic difference in that the former did not have a legally recognized relationship even though strong emotional ties might be forged.

Although milk kinship has been codified in Muslim law, the author describes several pre-Islamic examples of this behaviour which could be used to obtain friends and allies. Milk kinship was important for the Masai of Africa who would obtain lasting peace with an enemy tribe by exchanging cows and a woman from each tribe suckling a baby of the opposite tribe. In the Hindu Kush milk, or foster kinship as it was called, was maintained by ruling families producing ties between them which were more lasting than the ties of blood. In 19th century Georgia, Christian Georgians would send a newborn child to their Muslim trading partners in North Caucasia if the latter's wife was known to be breastfeeding. The Muslims would do the same, the purpose of which was to demonstrate the complete confidence of the parties concerned. The child would remain with the foster parents until aged 10 or 11, when it would be returned to the parents as proof that the child was not being used as cheap labour. Milk siblings would speak the same language, know the same traditions and when they reached adulthood were able to help each other with trade, transport and hospitality.

Milk kinship has to be seen within the general rules of kinship in Islam as this dictates to a large degree the kind of behaviour and social interaction which is allowable between individuals. Those who cannot marry because of kinship ties by blood, marriage or milk can mix freely, veiling of the women is not required and there is an easy familiarity in the relationship. Talking to older women who remembered from before the 1940s, when formula milk was introduced into Iran and the custom of milk kinship declined, it seems that a wet nurse/milk mother was only taken when it was considered absolutely essential. This was in cases such as when a mother died in childbirth, became ill or became pregnant again too quickly. There were no examples of the use of the relationship to prevent veiling or strict marriages. In fact, the Iranian's concern when practising the custom was to avoid the choice of person which could affect future marriage arrangements. It was difficult for these mothers to find a suitable person. The wet nurse had to be a person with the right moral and physical attributes. As this was likely to be a close friend of the family, who might have children who would in the future be marriage partners, they were not considered suitable because of the strictures of the milk kinship relationship.

Mothers were not on the whole willing for their baby to be taken to another woman's house and finding someone willing to 'live in' was generally difficult. A wet nurse who lived in the household had a lower status than one who did not as she was likely to come from a family where something had gone wrong so she could not continue living there. A wet nurse was considered of higher status than other servants but she was nevertheless considered to be just a servant. A non-resident wet nurse enjoyed a much higher status as she had her own family with whom she belonged. The fact that she was able to render such a valuable service to her higher-class neighbour put the latter in the position of being recipients rather than givers. A wet nurse in this position would not expect to get paid wages but would be given gifts instead. There were also cases of a higher-class family feeding the child of a lower-class one because this was considered a meritorious act.

The idea of milk kinship demonstrates the power of breast milk and the bond created between the breastfeeding mother and child. According to these traditional ideas, breast milk is a powerful substance which not only nurtures a growing baby physically but is also a symbol of the powerful forces that bind family members together.

PART TWO

PATTERNS OF
INFANT FEEDING

CHAPTER SIX

Unrestricted Breastfeeding

Why unrestricted breastfeeding?

Nowadays unrestricted breastfeeding is recommended as the best way for mothers to breastfeed. This means giving breast milk to babies when they are hungry rather than according to some prearranged schedule. In the west such 'new' advice comes after many years during which various types of schedules were imposed on breastfeeding mothers and their babies with disastrous effects.

Modern research has demonstrated how such schedules subvert the natural cycle by which the baby's appetite stimulates the mother's body in various ways to ensure that enough breast milk is produced (Woolridge and Baum, 1991). The more a baby sucks, the more the nipple is stimulated. This activates the hypothalamus in the brain which releases prolactin, the hormone responsible for making breast milk, and oxytocin, the hormone responsible for the release of the stored milk to the baby. At the same time there is a local inhibitory factor within the breast which causes the breast to fill more quickly just after being emptied and to inhibit breast milk production as the breast fills to capacity. This factor is triggered by the infant's appetite and, in particular, the extent to which this is satisfied by consuming not only a sufficient volume of milk but also sufficient milk with a high fat concentration. Breast milk which contains this high fat concentration is in the 'hind milk' available only after the baby has consumed the 'foremilk' at the start of feeding. If feeds are shortened, because of an externally imposed schedule, the baby will not get this fat rich milk which will make the baby feel hungry, hard to settle and will inhibit the production of milk in the future.

Mothers vary in the extent to which the overall bodily hormone pattern or the local breast hormone pattern of breast milk production is important to ensure sufficient milk for their baby. Different breastfeeding styles activate the hormone patterns differently and mothers need to experiment to find what is the most appropriate style for them and their baby, which may, of course, change as the baby grows. The best way to reach a balance between the baby's appetite and the right volume and composition of breast milk is to allow babies to suck as often and for as long as they like. Babies are clearly quite capable of self-regulating their own breast milk intake and, by doing so, enable mothers to create sufficient breast milk for their needs.

How unrestricted can unrestricted breastfeeding be?

In traditional communities unrestricted breastfeeding is the norm, and the style of baby care makes unrestricted breastfeeding more likely and possibly easier. Often mothers and babies are not expected to be separated during the first year or two of life. They are in close physical contact day and night with the baby being carried by the mother to wherever she is working and sleeping with her at night. Nevertheless, there are many traditional communities in which mothers and babies do have to be separated, sometimes for quite long periods during the day. Usually this is because of work, such as fetching water or firewood, for which mothers are responsible. Like mothers everywhere, mothers in traditional communities have a variety of sometimes conflicting demands on their time and energy especially, as often happens, they have the responsibility for growing the food that sustains their families. Although they may not be breastfeeding according to any kind of external schedule, the demands of their baby for food will have to be negotiated within this environment.

Mothers and babies in Mali (Dettwyler, 1987) are constantly together after birth and the baby is fed entirely on demand. Feeding according to any kind of schedule is unknown. Women say that whenever babies cry, this shows they are hungry and should be picked up and fed. Babies are therefore breastfed 'on demand' whenever they want and for as long as they like. It is considered imperative that a mother feeds her baby whenever he or she cries, if necessary stopping her work to do so. This is seen not as a burden or inconvenience but the baby's right. If a mother does try to ignore her baby's cries, she is strongly chastised by other people in the compound, even by strangers. So strong is this belief that a crying baby will be fed by a co-wife or grandmother if the mother is unavailable to do so. Babies are also given the breast for comfort which is considered just as important as food. Babies are not, however, offered the breast if they do not cry and are not woken up to feed, even if the mother's breasts are painfully full.

Throughout the day a woman's small baby is with her strapped to her back in a sling. Infants are held, usually by the mother, for at least 50 per cent of the time. To breastfeed, the mothers bring their babies round to the front of their bodies and hold them there while they feed. When the baby is older he or she sits on the mother's hip to feed. After the first few months, when babies can support their own heads, mothers do not give babies much support or attention while feeding. Babies find the breast for themselves and feed from it. Breastfeeding a baby does not, therefore, interrupt too much the other work in the fields and house that a mother has to do.

Babies can be observed feeding many times during the day and night and it was reported that few babies slept through the night until they were 12 months old or more. Mothers were not able to say how often or for how long they breastfed their babies but observation showed that nursing bouts were frequent and short, usually of about 15 minutes duration. Mothers estimated that they breastfed their babies 30 or more times in each 24-hour period and said this did not change until the child was about 12 months old. Babies and children stay physically close to their mothers until weaned. Even then, they continue to sleep close to their mother until they are five years old or so, after which they sleep with older children in another room.

Small babies are kept close to their mothers at all times in Mexico (Milliard and Graham, 1984) and they sleep together at night. Demand feeding is considered the only proper way to feed a child as only then can a mother be sure that her child will not go hungry. At the same time, breastfeeding is perceived as a process that needs conscious effort on the part of the mother, with the help of her family and friends, to produce milk of sufficient quality and quantity. Breastfeeding patterns are therefore heavily determined by maternal perceptions of the baby's needs – which can be expressed in ways other than crying – and as a result mothers do not routinely delay feeding until the child cries. The way the baby is carried around also affects to some degree the way they are fed. At the beginning of life the traditional swaddling techniques limit the child's self-initiated access to the breast. Later when the baby is carried on the mother's chest with hands free there is easier access. Then as the baby gets older and is carried on the mother's back, access is again somewhat limited. As a result of this there is not on the whole extremely frequent suckling, although in this study it was not investigated quantitatively. Other research carried out in a similar community found that up to the age of six months there was a great variety between different babies in the number and lengths of suckling. On average, however, for the first 18 months of life, babies were fed 12 times per day with around 200 minutes of suckling time.

In Guatemala (Solien de Gonzalez, 1963) babies are fed whenever they cry, whether during the day or night. Small babies sleep with their mothers who wake up and give them the breast if necessary, while older children simply take the breast themselves without having to wake the mother. Some children were reported to sleep with the nipple in their mouths, sucking now and then throughout the night. Gradually during the first year, babies suckle fewer times until they are taking the breast three to four times during the day and maybe once at night. By this time, when they are 8–12 months old, they are also eating some solid food. Most mothers reported that they had a good milk supply which needed no supplementation until the child was old enough to eat solid food.

Ideal mothering in the Amele community of Papua New Guinea (Jenkins, Orr-Ewing and Heywood, 1984) is very indulgent to the demands of babies and young children. A mother rarely refuses the breast to even an older child and breasts are often bitten and pulled while suckling and this is not considered unacceptable. Household tasks such as cooking are fitted around the demands of breastfeeding infants rather than the reverse and the demands of a breastfeeding baby are frequently cited as a reason for meals not being prepared on time. When the time comes for weaning, first attempts are always halfhearted with the mother refusing the breast to the child in public but often continuing to breastfeed in private. One reason for this may be because husbands are forbidden to sleep with their wives while they are still breastfeeding (although sexual intercourse can take place in other locations) and thus is a good excuse to avoid sex. Complete severance between the mother and her breastfeeding infant might not take place until the child is well over four years old, especially if the child is the last born or if the mother uses contraception.

One of the few studies to quantitatively examine unrestricted breastfeeding patterns in a less developed country was carried out in three rural villages in Madura, East Java, which is in Indonesia (van Steen-Bergen, Kusin, Sri Kardhati and Renqvist, 1991). Infant feeding patterns were studied longitudinally from birth to 52 weeks among all infants born in these villages between September 1982 and December 1984. Results showed that infants were nursed 'on demand' on an average of 15 times in 24 hours. The average daily time for suckling was 105–140 minutes in each 24 hours, 45 per cent of which took place at night between 6pm and 6am. The frequency of feeding was not influenced by age but the time spent suckling decreased from an average of 130 minutes in 24 hours at age 1–8 weeks to 95 minutes at age 25–32 weeks. The amount of milk ingested at each feed, however, was very similar throughout infancy as older infants were able to obtain the same amount of milk in a shorter sucking period. There was a tendency for those who were exclusively breastfed to suckle more frequently and for longer as well as taking more milk per feed. This tendency, however, was only significant for those aged one to eight weeks who took larger amounts of breast milk if they were exclusively breastfed. Among older infants, aged 37–56 weeks, breastfeeding frequency and intake were comparable to those of early infancy.

These results are very interesting in the light of the fact that all infants were given food other than breast milk from as early as the third day after birth. This consisted of local 'baby food' such as rice porridge but did not include a breast milk substitute. Research in modern industrial societies suggests that giving very young babies such food so early leads to shorter duration of breastfeeding. In this community, however, it seemed to have little effect either on the duration of breastfeeding or the average amount of breast milk which the babies consumed, which remained remarkably consistent throughout the first year of their lives. The authors speculate that perhaps amongst marginally nourished women such as those in this sample, frequency of suckling was the most important determinant of breast milk consumption. The higher milk intake of exclusively breastfed infants in the first few weeks of life was due to a higher yield per nursing and not a higher frequency of feeding. It was difficult to determine whether those who were exclusively breastfeeding during the first few weeks of life did so because their mothers' had a better milk supply or because the cultural mores concerning giving babies extra food were less strong.

It is often thought that women in traditional societies have work patterns and rhythms which are more in tune with breastfeeding. They are, therefore, more easily able to feed 'on demand' than those in western society who are more circumscribed by the clock. While there may be some truth in this assertion, it grossly oversimplifies the situation as was shown in research amongst breastfeeding mothers working in subsistence activities in Nepal (Panter-Brick, 1992). This study showed how not only work rhythms but the whole position of women in society influenced the 'unrestricted breastfeeding' of their children. It was carried out in a rural village and compared the experience of women from both the Tamang and Kami groups resident there. Although living in the same village, these two groups had different social characteristics and worked in different ways. The 233 Tamang families were of Tibetan-Burmo origin and the largest group in the village. They operated a mixed agro-pastoral economy of various crops at different elevations over the wide area of the mountainside on which they farmed. By contrast the 16 Kami families were of Indo-Aryan origin who had migrated from the plains some five generations previously. They worked as blacksmiths supplying the Tamang with agricultural and household implements in exchange for grain. The position of women within the two groups was quite different. The Tamang lifestyle was characterized by a flexible work schedule, little economic differentiation between households and a lack of rigid sexual division of labour within the family. The Tamang woman had a greater workload than the Kami woman and her labour was absolutely essential for the household's subsistence. Kami women did some work in agriculture and husbandry but this normally supplemented the blacksmith work of their husbands and so was not absolutely essential to the household economy. The expression of status for a Kami woman was to stay at home with children and this is what most of the older women did, sending out their younger dependants to work. By contrast the Tamang woman was valued for her work outside the home and women of all ages did this.

The economic activities of both groups of women were largely unaffected by pregnancy, although after birth both had a time of seclusion away from household and work responsibilities. To explore their breastfeeding behaviour while working, records were kept on a minute by minute basis of 58 village women. They were followed throughout the day (but not the night), each woman being observed for several days during four different seasons of the year. There was a marked seasonal variation of work input amongst Tamang mothers with a fourfold increase in work during the monsoon; households working individually or with a labour group at times of peak activity. Unexpectedly breastfeeding patterns appeared to differ very little according to the season or social context of the agricultural work. The demands of the young baby seemed to be satisfied whether the mother was working intensively during the monsoon, leisurely during the winter months or working individually or within a group. While the work performance of breastfeeding women differed from other women in the more leisurely winter months, similar time inputs of work were observed during the intensive monsoon period. Breastfeeding mothers did work slightly shorter hours in the fields but mostly they scheduled their nursing sessions during work breaks to minimize interference from children in their work. Usually mothers breastfed their babies while other women were resting and eating. Despite possible interference from their breastfeeding babies, mothers were reckoned to contribute the same amount of labour as other members of the workforce, the contribution of a day's work being accepted whether the mother was old, young, pregnant or breastfeeding.

By contrast the Kami women had less work to do in the fields, particularly during the monsoon season. They went less frequently outside the village and travelled around in a more circumscribed area on the mountain side. Their subsistence activities were not modified by current pregnant and breastfeeding behaviour but were influenced by differences in age and household status. A woman's workload amongst this group was an expression of her status which improved with age and the birth of many children. Thus older women with many children would stay at home, sending the younger members of the household out to do the work in the fields. Tamang women usually took their children with them in their work until they were too heavy to carry when they would be left at home with older siblings. Kami women, because they did not have so much work to do outside the house, tended to leave their babies at home, often leaving the baby's cot in the smithy. When the baby cried the father would ask one of the other children to go and get the mother so she could feed the child. In all it was found that Tamang mothers breastfed an average of nine times per day with a suckling time of 65 minutes, two-thirds of feeds (68 per cent) occurring during the completion of her subsistence activities. Kami mothers fed an average of 9.4 times per day for a total of 60 minutes while only a third (38 per cent) of feeds took place during the mother's outdoor activities. Thus breastfeeding patterns were very similar despite the different kinds of work and different involvement of women with work outside the home.

The quantified observations obtained in this research validated the concepts of 'demand' or 'opportunity' feeding which had been observed and reported in the anthropological literature. At the same time work patterns were important determinants of child care with the type of activity governing the mother's availability for breastfeeding. Work patterns also governed the availability of substitute caretakers. Although child care might interfere with a woman's work, a nursing mother was still counted as a full member of the workforce and little attention was paid to potential or individual differences in labour input because she was breastfeeding. There was no discrimination against the nursing mother amongst the Tamang mainly because of the urgent demand for labour for subsistence tasks. What was of potential importance to child health was what happened as the child became too heavy to carry around. Tamang women, with their greater outside responsibilities which took them away from the house for long periods, left such children with older siblings to be looked after. At very busy times of the year, younger children were as a result somewhat neglected with consequent poorer health. This was less of a problem for Kami women who had less outside responsibilities and more adults at home to care for the child when it was necessary.

Although mothers from traditional communities apparently respond readily to their baby's demands for food at any time of the day or night, this does not take place in a vacuum. Practical factors, such as how the mother works and how the baby is dressed and carried, will affect it. Also the breastfeeding needs of the baby have to be satisfied within a network of sometimes conflicting demands and attitudes on the mother. Cultural norms about the extent to which the baby's need for food could and should be indulged and take precedence over the demands of other family members are also important. A mother's breastfeeding style reflects many aspects of her environment.

The place of the clock in breastfeeding

Now that we have 'discovered' unrestricted breastfeeding in the west, the differences between breastfeeding styles in traditional and modern societies are much less glaring than they used to be. When anthropologists came from societies where babies were supposed to feed according to an externally imposed schedule, many of them made comments of surprise on what they saw as a somewhat exotic way of feeding babies. Now that the benefits of unrestricted breastfeeding are understood, comment is made about the long period in the west when externally imposed schedules on baby feeding were the norm. Given the catastrophic effects such schedules had on breastfeeding, even when breastfeeding was being encouraged, it must be asked why such schedules were in vogue for so long.

An analysis of paediatric literature on breastfeeding during the 20th century (Millard, 1991) provides an interesting insight into the rationales given for various schedules and highlights the place of the clock within them. The history of birth during the 20th century is the history of how birth became progressively more medicalized and hospital-based. All too often women were encouraged to ignore their own bodily signals while pregnant and giving birth, these being interpreted as misleading or irrelevant compared to measurement by machines. Many women came to breastfeeding after an experience of birth which included an intense experience of ignoring their bodily signals which were defined as problems rather than guides to action. Not surprisingly, when it came to breastfeeding, they turned to external pointers for what they should do rather than listening to their own internal signals. This reinforced the power of the hospital in shaping early breastfeeding experience and health care professionals, rather than other experienced women, became authorities. During the 20th century women became more and more dependent on advice from professionals about breastfeeding and were less and less likely to have watched another woman breastfeed before trying to do so themselves.

Despite the increasingly powerful postpartum position of health professionals, the connection from paediatric advice to actual breastfeeding is complex and not completely understood. Various studies have shown that professional advice on its own is not an important factor in determining whether a mother initiates breastfeeding or not. Rather it depends on the congruence of breastfeeding with other aspects of a woman's life and her ideas about her baby's nutrition, with kin, social network, class and subculture being other important factors. Paediatric advice does, however, seem to be sought and does have some effect on practice even if, as studies have shown, women modify the advice to suit their own situations.

The advice in the paediatric manuals showed there to be a contradiction, sometimes explicit but more often implicit, between flexibility and rigid structuring. All the sources criticize excess rigidity but continue to structure their advice with timetables that contradict the principle of flexibility. These contradictions, although easy to spot now, were not evident to the physicians of the time. They could be evidence of struggles to integrate past rigidities with present flexibilities, as well as attempting to recognize complexity while emerging with simple, easily given advice. Looking specifically at advice on how long babies should be allowed to suck, for example, authors acknowledge that individual babies can be very different and need to feed for different lengths of time. At the same time, however, they also state that a baby should not be left to suck on the breast beyond a certain length of time and most give a specific time for how long a baby should be allowed to suck.

The length of the interval between feeds received a good deal of attention. The idea that babies should be fed at regular intervals has remained in place over decades, although the rationales and recommended times between feeds has changed. From early to mid-century, advice changed from suggesting that babies were fed at two-hourly intervals to intervals of four or five hours. The rationale for this was that scheduling prevented digestive illnesses. Some books blamed high rates of infant mortality on feeding procedures in the home and made it the mother's duty to keep to a feeding schedule which lessened this possibility. Congruent with the biomedical approach of these authors, breastfeeding was discussed only in physical, almost mechanistic terms. The milk producer was 'the breast' rather than 'the mother' and whatever schedules were suggested were based on hospital/clinical knowledge rather than bodily experience.

Timetables

The concept of rigid feeding schedules may well have originated in the hospital nursery where work was organized on schedules and efficiency was of prime importance. The invention of breastfeeding schedules also served as a basis of physicians assertion of expertise. The evolution of timetables has continued to reinforce the ascendancy of paediatric advice over that of ordinary women. Economic considerations should not be overlooked for, as the formula companies have continually reiterated to physicians, directing the routine of infant feeding is a good source of income. At the same time it was thought that infants needed discipline through an external schedule to accustom their nervous systems to certain times for food, rest and play. Earlier sources saw this as a start on the way to responsible adulthood. Generations of mothers tried to follow these instructions and, in doing so, undermined the breastfeeding cycle making it difficult, if not impossible, to breastfeed successfully. It is difficult to correlate specific advice with declines in breastfeeding but such schedules probably led to insufficient breast milk and increased infant hunger. In suggesting such feeding programmes, paediatricians indirectly promoted bottle feeding.

By the middle of the century paediatric texts had begun to discuss 'natural feeding schedules' and 'infant designed schedules' as workable options. By the late 1960s texts were referring to 'demand feeding' which has been widely recommended since the early 1970s. The definition of 'demand', however, was somewhat ambiguous. In one source it meant a vocal signal from the baby and in another outright crying. Surprisingly, however, the expectation of a feeding schedule was maintained together with a justification for not feeding too often as this could inhibit the production of the hormone that produces breast milk (in fact the reverse is true; the more the baby sucks, the more milk will be produced). There is thus the contradiction that, although the infant should be allowed to feed 'on demand', this must not be too frequent otherwise the baby will have poor eating habits and the mother poor milk production. One text is quoted which at one point says mothers should allow their baby to nurse when hungry but at another point says that frequent small feeding to pacify all crying should not be cultivated! Thus demand feeding is alright but only up to a point.

These medical texts also assume that some form of regularity on the part of the baby is a normal part of infant behaviour. Eventually it is expected that the baby will conform to some kind of schedule, although this will derive from the baby's internal needs rather than be imposed from outside. A mother is advised to feed 'on demand' but to expect that her baby will eventually maintain a regular sequence of feeding spaced well apart. Individual variation must ultimately be framed by a schedule, despite the fact there is evidence which shows that regular meals are not necessarily a part of normal infant behaviour. A few recent paediatric texts do depart from the idea that feeding schedules are fundamental. None suggest, however, that unrestricted breastfeeding can take place as part of a negotiation between mother and child so that the needs of both can be meshed together for the satisfaction of both.

The clock is a central theme related to breastfeeding in 20th century paediatric literature but has undergone a major shift. During the earlier decades of the century, the literature portrayed the infant as needing an introduction to a scheduled life as soon as possible. This ensured right from the beginning that they would be subject to the constraints of the clock, which in the future would be necessary for their competence as adults in holding jobs and living with others. Since women were mostly excluded from the work world, where such schedules were the norm, they were perceived as needing discipline and professional guidance from paediatricians concerning the appropriateness of various schedules. By the 1960s, however, the view that infants needed to be trained to live by an externally imposed schedule was superseded by today's perspective that the timetable is an innate characteristic of normal infants. Thus paediatric authorities now advocate what is considered 'normal' for infants in terms of how long and how often they breastfeed. The clock has moved from the realm of culture as perceived in science, training and discipline to that of nature and organic processes. It has moved from outside to inside the human body.

These shifts indicate not only a new ethno-anatomy on the part of physicians but also a different view of human nature by the society at large. The clock, having been internalized, is now thought to be inherent in human behaviour. Schedules are considered necessary for many activities such as work, sports, leisure, family life and have become a standard for judging competence, adequacy and normality. Thus the expectation that babies will conform to a feeding timetable, even though it may derive from their internal needs, is a reflection of a general cultural expectation that all behaviour is governed by schedules. The clock is at the core of many cultural themes and it is not surprising that it is still considered to be a fundamental element of infant feeding, even though the way that it is described has changed.

The conflict between schedules as promoted by the paediatrician and the baby's own rhythms was shown very graphically in research carried out in Turin, Italy (Balsalmo, 1992). The mothers in this sample had their babies in the 1970s and 1980s and gave birth in hospitals and clinics, so that what happened in the hospital immediately after birth was a constant feature of the interviews. Nearly all these mothers were separated from their baby after birth (seen as a modern 'rite of passage' by these authors). The mother had to lie in bed after delivery and her baby was brought to her at regular times. The difficulty that many women had under these conditions of feeling active and responsible for their baby and able to meet their baby's needs may have been one obstacle to achieving successful breastfeeding. It appeared that three main figures directed and controlled the mother's breastfeeding behaviour:

- the mother's mother;
- the hospital which set down the essential rules of breastfeeding; and,
- the paediatrician who kept a check on things.

Husbands, although sometimes helpful and playing an important role just after the birth, did not appear to have an important role in the long-term.

Many mothers were given either no advice and help about breastfeeding or incorrect advice by the hospital staff. In the hospital, breastfeeding was under the control of the medical staff and mothers were expected to adhere to a hospital routine which included what could be described as modern rituals, such as disinfecting their nipples before feeding, feeding for only a certain amount of time and test weighing after every feed to make sure the baby had eaten 'enough'. If the baby had not (as defined by hospital norms), he or she was given supplementary food in a bottle. In many cases this not unsurprisingly led to a vicious supplementary feeding circle that inhibited breastfeeding. The baby did not suck 'enough' in the time allowed and was given a supplementary feed. He or she was sleepy at the next feed so sucked even less and may have fallen asleep, thus inhibiting the flow of milk from the mother. In the meantime the woman's breasts became engorged with milk which the staff dealt with by using a breast pump. Many women disliked this intensely, seeing it as yet another assault on their bodies, which were being treated like machines – and imperfect machines at that. The mother emptied her breast with a breast pump while her baby, unable to get at the milk, was being fed a questionable surrogate for the real thing.

The quantitative and visual version of the child's well-being was the only accepted standard in the hospital. Any indicators of emotional and physical sensitivity between mother and child were discounted. This standard derived not only from the medical culture of the hospital but also the interplay between various units and centres of power in the hospital. At birth the health of the baby passed from the concern of the obstetrician to that of the paediatrician who often focused exclusively on the baby without considering the mother. The control of breastfeeding given to the medical staff was separated from the woman breastfeeding. The only acceptable signs of well-being for the breastfed child were quantitative. The mother was treated as a milk machine and if the baby didn't grow or ingest milk according to a pre-determined norm, then extra milk was given from a bottle.

The hospitals said that babies should be fed every three-and-a-half hours and mothers returned home expecting to implement this schedule there. For most it was difficult to achieve and few were able to reproduce the rhythms of hospital in the home. Of those who continued breastfeeding, most ended up more or less with demand feeding. Those mothers who spoke of breastfeeding with satisfaction did not keep to rigid timetables and prolonged the length of feeding time compared to what had been advised by the doctors. They seemed to be able to accept and enjoy the subtle breastfeeding relationship between mother and baby that the paediatricians did not wish to recognize. The authors hypothesize that it is this kind of attachment that the social control of breastfeeding, as exemplified in the schedules of paediatricians, aims at restricting and preventing. Some paediatricians consciously deplored any tendency of erotic relationship between mother and the breastfeeding infant. As a result they said that feeds should not be no more than a few minutes long, thus making successful breastfeeding even less likely. This is in tune with the Catholic church, which sanctions the repression of pleasure in women and substitutes it with the myth of a chaste long-suffering love for the child.

A theme which emerged from discussion of breastfeeding management was that of attachment versus detachment. When the tendency was toward attachment, mothers prolonged their togetherness with their child as long as possible and delayed the moment of separation. Their child was perceived as an 'other', with wishes of his or her own which should be respected. When the baby cried this was the way he or she expressed his or her needs. The mother placed herself on the same level as the child and tried to meet his or her wishes, even though at times this could lead to a state of conflict. A mother who expressed a desire for detachment (which was more typical of middle-class mothers) sought independence both for herself and her child. For this group, breastfeeding was an opportunity to educate and socialize the baby in the right way for his or her own good. Crying was an opportunity for the baby to learn a lesson.

Some mothers, however, who went home with every intention of keeping to the schedule as laid down by the specialist, often found that it was broken by the brute force of the baby's crying. In this situation the role of the paediatrician was often that of defending the mother from excessive encroachment of child and supporting her attempts to impose a schedule. Whatever the mother's relationship with the paediatrician, and some turned away from him as soon as they left hospital, none escaped completely the quantitative criteria which was a hallmark of the paediatrician's work. Checking the child's health was carried out almost exclusively, using quantitative means such as test feeds and weighing the baby which the authors felt were a measure of social control rather than measurement per se. The relation of subject and object (mother and baby) being mediated by an instrument (the scales) kept women in a state of cultural, material and symbolic dependency on the (usually male) doctor. This social control over breastfeeding also acted as a restraint which neutralized female sexual expression and pleasure and undermined the formation of ties between mother and baby that might threaten the social organization based on privilege for adult males.

As the authors point out, quantitative criteria associating time schedules and quantity with breastfeeding corresponds to a model of industrial and economic planning, which deals with every problem in terms of how scarce resources, including time, are to be combined for efficiency. 'Optimum breastfeeding' was a model of efficiency, not pleasure. For women, accepting this terminology and view of things involved becoming alienated from their bodies which they experienced as outside objects. The decision-making was carried out by the doctor as to how and when the baby should be fed and the mothers were merely the means by which this was accomplished. In such a situation breastfeeding can be seen as a social preparation for the ordering of time in our culture. Some mothers thought that such rules were part of a genetic heritage and that a baby should feed according to some kind of schedule. When this did not happen, breastfeeding was experienced as never ending and exhausting because it went against the perception that such scheduling is a fundamental aspect of human behaviour.

The authors conclude by showing that much of the conflict experienced by these mothers developed during a particular experience of time, derived from industrial/patriarchal society, which was imposed on their experience. Breastfeeding is a primary experience which is outside normal 'social' conceptions of time. When time schedules are imposed on this, conflict within the mother is inevitable as the two conceptions of time are fundamentally at odds.

The idea between 'natural time' and 'social time' is, I feel, of crucial importance and needs to be understood by everyone who supports breastfeeding. 'Natural time', as it applies to breastfeeding, is related to the cycles of a mother's and baby's body and how they relate through the medium of breastfeeding, while 'social time' is defined by a focus on the clock. Often the two are incompatible and to breastfeed successfully mothers need the space to tune into the former rather than the latter. While I was breastfeeding, I found that to respond to the needs of my baby and her rhythms was like taking 'time out of mind' and to fall into a completely different state of consciousness and perception of time. For me it often seemed that I inhabited different universes where it was more or less impossible to fit the two kinds of cycles together.

This was shown to me very graphically when, two days after Emma's birth, the midwife asked me how often I had fed my newborn the previous day. 'I don't know', I replied, hurriedly changing this to 'well probably at least six times', when I saw the midwife's face fall at this first 'wrong' answer. The real truth was that I neither knew nor cared as this seemed to be a totally irrelevant question within this state of consciousness, where I felt very connected to my baby and responsive to her needs. I fed my daughter when she was hungry and the kind of tuning in that I was doing with her and my body made counting irrelevant. Similarly I really didn't know for how long she sucked. She just sucked until she had had enough and it wasn't part of my consciousness to time her. I often found it a strain trying to fit these two cycles together, not only because they were often at odds with each other from a practical point of view, but that the tuning in to the more subtle signals of my baby and my body was difficult when there were so many external signals clamouring for attention. My baby had rhythms which were often quite incompatible with the clock and I could see how many women could so easily give up the difficult struggle of trying to integrate the two, especially when the clock demands, by which the rest of the family lived, could feel so imperative.

CHAPTER SEVEN

Supplemented Breastfeeding

Traditional breast milk supplements

Advice to mothers nowadays is to feed their babies for the first four to six months of their lives exclusively on breast milk (Enkin, Keirse, Renfrew and Neilson, 1996; Smale, 1992). There is, it seems, no physiological advantage to be gained by giving any kind of supplements during these first months, whether of water, formula or solids. In fact, such supplements can interfere with the development of the baby's immature immune system and also decreases the length of time that mothers will continue to breastfeed. Women whose babies receive routine supplements are up to five times more likely to give up breastfeeding in the first week, and twice as likely to abandon it in the second week as those with babies who do not receive supplements. In many traditional communities, however, exclusive breastfeeding for this length of time is rare. I have been unable to carry out a systematic survey of different cultures, but given the widespread practice of supplemented breastfeeding I wonder if this, rather than exclusive breastfeeding, is the norm, especially in communities where mothers are only marginally nourished. As already described, pre-lacteal feeding is very common and in many places babies are given other food as well as breast milk from a very early age. Unlike the west, however, this seems to go with both a high incidence and long duration of breastfeeding.

Sometimes views about the nature of the baby's physical body and/or digestion will determine whether and what supplements are given in addition to breast milk. In Peru (Wellin, 1955), a baby is given an occasional bottle of milk from the first months as part of a gradual initiation away from the breast. The milk is always boiled, not for hygienic purposes but because it is a 'cold food' and therefore bad for the infant unless it has been heated up. During early infancy until some time during the sixth and 12th month, the baby receives only milk except for herb tea or sugared water. Reasons given for this are that the infant's body is considered to be delicate, to 'lack resistance' and that solid foods are 'too strong' for the assumed frailty of the infant's stomach. The prime needs of infant nutrition during the first months of life are to build up the infant's resistance so that he or she can ingest solid food. This is thought to be best achieved with an unsupplemented milk, but not necessarily breast milk, diet. By itself milk is a 'good' food but with other items it is potentially harmful. Drunk before or after eating fruit, sweets, heavy or cold foods it produces an antagonistic mixture in the stomach which provokes a 'bilious' reaction. For this reason, the introduction of both animal milk and solid food into a baby's diet is done very gradually so that the body is not shocked by suddenly having to cope with something new.

In Papua New Guinea, Amele mothers (Jenkins, Orr-Ewing and Heywood, 1984), usually within the first week of birth, gave their newborn the warmed juice of a ripe papaya so the child does not cry from hunger. A baby is considered hungry if he or she cries after being breastfed or chews on the mother's nipples. If this happens soups and juices are given to the baby, but when the mother is convinced that 'stronger' milk has developed in her breasts, these supplements are discontinued. As in many traditional communities, child nutrition is child-led and unless a child cries and/or points to food, it will not be given anything other than breast milk, sometimes for up to eight to ten months.

Giving various sorts of supplementary food to young babies was found to be widespread in a study carried out in India (Chandrashekar, 1985). Here, amongst a sample of 300 mothers from various economic backgrounds, only 15 per cent of babies aged three to five months old were exclusively breastfed, the rest being given supplementary milk or food. In the sample as a whole just over two thirds (67 per cent) were regularly giving their babies diluted cow's milk as a supplement to breast milk. Supplementary milk was introduced by 14 per cent of mothers in the first month, 24 per cent in the second month and 50 per cent in the third month of child's life. It seemed that the college educated mothers were more likely to be reading books and to be more influenced by health personnel about the benefits of exclusive breastfeeding. In this sample all such mothers continued breastfeeding, 25 per cent doing so exclusively, compared to a lesser number of mothers with less formal education in the other three groups. Three-quarters of babies were also being given water regularly at the time of the interview but mothers had no definite reasons for doing so.

Research carried out on supplemented breastfeeding in traditional communities has usually focused on the quantitative effects this has on breastfeeding, rather than seeking explanations as to why this is the preferred infant feeding style. This was explored, for instance, in a comparative study carried out in Kenya and Indonesia (Kusin, Kardjati, van Steenbergen, 1985). In Kenya, mothers breastfed their babies exclusively for two to three months or longer. At that age complementary foods consisting of cow's milk, maize and flour gruel were introduced, these being gradually replaced by the family diet of maize, beans and vegetables towards the end of the first year. By contrast, in Madur, Indonesia, babies were fed things other than breast milk from as young as one week, mashed bananas and boiled rice being the most popular food. In this community rice was considered the only good food for infants up to the age of nine months; pulses, fish and vegetables were seldom offered even at the end of infancy.

Why did Indonesian mothers offer other food to their babies so early in their lives? Unfortunately the mothers were not very explicit about this, maybe because of the constraints of the mainly quantitative research methodology. Reasons given included that the infant often cried or that by giving the baby more food he or she would grow larger. This need to have the child 'larger' was, the researchers thought, a need to have an 'older' child which meant that the mother could leave the child with someone else and resume normal duties outside the home as early as possible. The researchers wondered if such early introduction of supplementary food increased the risk of diarrhoea in young babies. In fact diarrhoea in young babies under the age of six months was less common in Kenya than Indonesia, but the data was insufficient to determine whether this was owing to the protective effects of exclusive breastfeeding or some other factor. Physiologically speaking the early introduction of weaning foods should also give shorter duration of postpartum amenorrhoea (the time between birth and when menstruation begins) and it would therefore be expected that Indonesian mothers would have babies closer together. In fact this was not so, and in both places to have a pregnancy within 12 months of a birth was the exception.

The growth of the babies faltered around the third month in Indonesia, but not in Kenya and it was difficult to find an explanation for this. It could be because the supplementary food given by the Indonesian mothers brought about more illness among their children, who as a result lost weight, especially when mothers felt they had to discontinue breastfeeding if their children were not well. One interesting result was that the energy intake from breast milk consumed (calculated by test weighing babies) was not influenced by whether infants received complementary foods or not. It seemed that however much non-breast milk food was being consumed, the average breast milk intake for infants between the ages of one and six months was about the same (700ml/day).

More detail about the types of supplementary food given to Indonesian babies included evidence (van Steenbergen, Kusin, Kardjati and Renqvist, 1991) that mashed banana was the food of preference given to the newborn during the first week of life. This was replaced by mashed banana and rice as the baby grew older, and followed by soft rice (infant nasi). A few infants were eating the family rice and maize mixture before the age of 28 weeks. An egg, fish or vegetable side dish was taken by about 30 per cent of infants at around one year of age. Usually infants were offered food twice a day with infant rice being consumed by 84–100 per cent of infants at age 1–32 weeks. Infants who ate rice ingested 20–50gm per day. At late infancy and around one year of age nearly three-quarters of children were eating 45–55gm of this rice each day. Apart from rice, 'infant nasi' and banana, other foods were rarely eaten.

Breast milk substitutes, however, were hardly ever used and throughout infancy breast milk was the major source of protein. On average it seemed that the amounts consumed were comparable from early to late infancy. The mean intake of energy and protein from additional foods increased substantially between the first and second month and thereafter there was a slight increase up to 20 weeks which remained equal at best up to 30 weeks. As in Kenya it was found that there was no relationship between energy intake from additional foods and breast milk intake between one and 24 weeks, with breast milk consumption remaining the same regardless of how such supplementary food was being given. As the baby grew older this changed, as at age 25–32 weeks energy intake from additional foods had a significant negative association with milk intake and number of feeds.

A similar study which examined both the content and energy value of supplementary food was carried out in Thailand (Jackson, 1992). Here it was found that 13 per cent of the sample of 62 infants received their first food other than breast milk within seven days of birth and most of the infants (81 per cent) had been given supplementary food by six weeks of age (this did not include pre-lacteal feeds). The median age of introduction was four weeks. Some 18 per cent of mothers, however, did not immediately continue feeding supplements after introducing them for the first time. In most cases the first food other than breast milk was rice based. Glutinous rice, with its higher energy density, was preferred to ordinary rice although there were 211 different kinds of supplementary food given to the infants in this sample during the first year of life. At 2–6 weeks of age, the supplementary diet consisted mostly of mashed rice and banana, or rice alone, but infant formula, commercial infant cereal and fresh fruit juice were also given. By six months of age, all infants were receiving supplements of some kind. Mashed rice and banana was still popular but the major new component was meat and eggs. By six months of age, 45 per cent of infants had meat in their diets and fresh fruit was also very common. At 9–12 months old, mashed banana and rice was phased out with an increasing consumption of meat dishes. There were also a lot of different snacks being consumed.

Up to three months of age supplements contributed 7–14 per cent of total daily energy intake in those infants supplemented. The percentage of infants receiving more than one-quarter of their daily energy intake from supplements was 11 per cent at two weeks, 8 per cent at six weeks and 21 per cent at three months. By six months supplementary food contributed one-third (33 per cent) of the daily energy intake, at nine months nearly a half (47 per cent) and at 12 months nearly two-thirds (59 per cent). Energy intakes exceeded guidelines for healthy children in affluent societies but was 10–12 per cent less than recommended for infants age 6–12 months by WHO. Analysis showed that supplementary foods were introduced earlier if the infant was born in a large household, in a remoter part of the study area and to mothers in farming families. There was a tendency for older mothers to be more likely to give supplementary food and also those with girls and babies of lower birthweight. Supplementary food was thus probably introduced for a number of practical reasons, as well as to follow traditional patterns.

The researchers conclude that the timing of supplementary feeding and types of food given were part of a pattern of giving babies breast milk along with other food which is widespread throughout Southeast Asia. The nutritional quality of the supplementary food was high and provided a good variety of food in the second half of the first year of life. They compared these results to data from Bangladesh where only five per cent of infants aged 12 months had ever had meat or fish. Despite early supplementation, breastfeeding was prolonged with a median duration 12 months; seven per cent of mothers were still breastfeeding at 24 months. This was not because of the size of supplements given as, even when supplements were supplying 50 per cent of the energy requirements of 30 day old infants, breastfeeding continued for a long time. Unlike in the west, early supplementation was not associated with shorter duration of breastfeeding.

The distinction between formula and traditional supplements and their effect on breastfeeding seemed to be important. The eight mothers who offered infant formula to their infants had slightly shorter lactation time than those offering traditional foods. Maybe mothers intending to breastfeed for a shorter period, or who were less enthusiastic about breastfeeding, may have deliberately started their infants on formula. It is also possible that formula given by bottle and teat, for physiological reasons, may have competed against breastfeeding more effectively than food by spoon or hand.

Advice on infant feeding in developing countries has focused on promoting exclusive breastfeeding in the first 4–6 months for nutritional reasons and also as a birth spacing mechanism. As these studies show, however, to give this kind of advice is at variance with many traditional practices. Any confusion that a mother may feel about doing this may lead to the cessation of breastfeeding as a way of resolving such conflicts, especially if she can afford breast milk substitutes. Giving this kind of advice may therefore inadvertently lead to less breastfeeding. One problem is to recognize at what point breast milk will no longer meet infant's nutritional needs and when solid food should be introduced. Although general guidelines can be given, babies are very individual in this respect so that any advice must necessarily be in very general terms. In any case, the timing of supplementary feeds could be very resistant to change. Breastfeeding advice might, therefore, be more effective if it takes local customs and constraints into account rather than trying to lay down a completely new set of guidelines. Public health programmes, which emphasize the maintenance of breastfeeding in conjunction with hygienic preparation and storage of supplementary foods, may be more successful in promoting infant health than those that try to impose a completely different regime of infant feeding which is at odds with local practices.

Traditional supplements and modern substitutes

Patterns of traditional supplementation and the effects of the introduction of modern breast milk substitutes was explored in a study that compared changing patterns of infant feeding in Malaysia, Caribbean, Nigeria and Zaire (King and Ashworth, 1987). In these countries colostrum was traditionally rejected and pre-lacteal feeds were given instead. In each of the countries reviewed, supplemented breastfeeding was the norm and in none was exclusive breastfeeding for 4–6 months a universal practice; in all places prolonged breastfeeding was usual, together with supplementation with food and fluids other than breast milk from the first weeks of life. The reasons for this early supplementation, however, varied. In some cases it was thought that a baby was hungry and in need of supplementary food owing to a perceived insufficiency of breast milk. In some communities the staple food, whether rice or maize, was considered the strength giving component of the diet and babies were considered to need this as much as adults. During the period investigated, many mothers wanted to accustom their baby to other food in preparation for their return to work on plantation or farm.

The change away from these traditional patterns began early in the 20th century in Malaysia and the Caribbean, in the 1960s in Nigeria and in the 1980s, when this study was undertaken, most mothers in Zaire were still keeping to their traditional feeding practices. In Malaysia the feeding of milk from bottles was reported as early as 1920 amongst wealthy mothers, for whom it was fashionable and amongst the poorer mothers, particularly rubber plantation workers, for whom it was a necessity to work. By the 1950s there was almost universal initiation of breastfeeding but supplements were introduced at an early age. During this time there was a trend away from the traditional supplements of cooked bananas and rice towards wheat-flour products and patent cornflower. Since the 1950s, the duration of breastfeeding has declined substantially in urban areas but initiation has been little affected. In rural Malaysia there has been no decline in initiation and only a modest decline in duration. The use of artificial milk has increased, particularly in urban areas and early supplementation with non-milk supplements continues to be common. Commercial baby cereals are increasingly popular for very young infants and are replaced by traditional cereals toward the end of the first year.

During the period of slavery in the Caribbean, the traditional African practice of prolonged breastfeeding was thought to be against the interests of the slave owners. A period of breastfeeding not exceeding 16 months was therefore recommended. One writer advised that mothers could return to work one month after giving birth and that babies could be given supplements by the creche attendants between the breaks allowed for breastfeeding. At the beginning of the 20th century, early supplementation was still common using arrowroot porridge, bread slops with sugar and/or milk. In the 1940s and 50s, there was still universal initiation of breastfeeding and most mothers breastfed for over a year. At the same time early supplementation of breastfeeding continued with herb teas, milk, if the mother could afford it, and porridges of cornmeal, oatmeal and arrowroot. In the late 1950s and 60s, the overall duration of breastfeeding had been reduced to nine months and supplementation with milk was observed from as early as three months. From the mid 1960s, although the initiation of breastfeeding was almost universal, there was considerable variation in breastfeeding duration between urban and rural areas. In three studies undertaken during this time it was found that fewer than 50 per cent of urban mothers breastfed for six months or more. There was little change in duration of breastfeeding in rural areas but a greater use of artificial milks was observed.

In Nigeria one of the first studies on breastfeeding carried out in a large town in Western Nigeria found that only 13 per cent of mothers had ever used artificial milk. By the late 1950s and early 60s, however, partial bottle feeding with artificial milk, water or gruel was becoming increasingly common. This was especially so among mothers from elite groups among whom the duration of breastfeeding was reducing. Since then, while the initiation of breastfeeding has continued to be universal, there has been a slight decline in breastfeeding among low income women. Artificial milk has become widely used in urban areas and there is a trend towards early introduction, with usage peaking when the baby is aged six months and followed by a gradual decline. In the past decade, supplementation in the first three months has been with artificial (dried) milk with infant formula being increasingly used. It seems that traditional supplements are still the most popular non-milk food, although people who can afford them use commercial cereals.

In each of the countries examined, the work of health workers has had a variable impact on breastfeeding. Milk distribution programmes were a mixed blessing; they provided a short-term answer to a pressing need for hungry mothers and babies but they created a demand which could not necessarily be guaranteed in the long-term. Milk products were offloaded as food aid in times of surplus, while recipient countries were left to purchase them at high market prices during times of scarcity. Also, by distributing milk to infants from welfare centres, Government health services inadvertently endorsed artificial feeding thus promoting bottle feeding.

The relative importance of female employment varied. In Malaysia and the Caribbean this factor was responsible for the early shift towards supplementation with processed milk, which for working women was considered easier and more nutritious than traditional supplements. In Nigeria, however, the traditional roles of women, whether farming, trading or in purdah were compatible with exclusive breastfeeding, the period of which was longer than in Malaysia or the Caribbean. In Zaire, where mothers are often inadequately nourished as well as having to leave the house for long periods each day to tend their small farms, traditional forms of supplementation continue. In both the latter countries where women have joined the non-traditional labour force, however, a decline in breastfeeding can be seen.

In each of the developing countries reviewed, many, if not most, breastfeeding mothers have traditionally given supplements to their children at an early age because of economic responsibilities, a perceived insufficiency of breast milk and/or cultural attitudes towards colostrum and staple foods. This pattern of early supplementation has continued but there has been a change from using traditional food to commercially prepared items, either formula or various kinds of weaning food. It does appear that there has been a decline in breastfeeding duration in Malaysia and the Caribbean and, to a lesser extent, in Nigeria. This changed behaviour is associated with the same factors associated with a similar change of behaviour in western countries, namely urbanization, increased female participation in the workforce, increased availability of processed milk and their promotion both by companies and the health sector and the regimentation of breastfeeding. In all countries initiation rates for breastfeeding continue to be high but the duration of breastfeeding is diminishing, especially in urban areas where employment in the modern labour sector seems to be incompatible with breastfeeding.

The impact of formula on infant feeding practices and its perceived value as compared to breast milk was apparent in a study carried out in Bangladesh (Blanchet, 1991). Out of 108 mothers interviewed, nearly half (42 per cent) had introduced supplementary feeding by the time the child was two months old and a third had done so in the first month of life. Often this came about if the baby cried and did not seem to be appeased by the breast or anything that anyone could do. This situation created a great deal of anxiety because the baby's crying was interpreted as a sign that there was a spirit around who wanted the baby. Amulets were obtained but families would also readily feed their babies food other than breast milk to pacify them and thus keep evil spirits away.

Amongst these mothers breast milk as a 'natural' product did not have same status as commercial food. Supplementary food of all sorts was bought by men (who were generally responsible for the marketing) with money which gave such food more prestige. The researchers gave the example of what happened in a family when a son was born after four daughters and was therefore the object of special rejoicing: a tin of milk powder was bought for the baby by the extended family which was considered a very special gift which the mother proudly displayed. Generally it was felt that although breast milk was good for a normally healthy child, for a superior, above average baby supplementary food was needed. There seemed to be contradictory beliefs that breast milk was both inadequate and essential, but it was unclear whether this had always been the case or whether modern advertising of breast milk substitutes and weaning food was responsible.

It was believed that a small baby could eat only sugary food and often the first food other than breast milk was palm sugar dissolved in hot water. Other food including cow's milk was perceived as too 'strong'. Sugar was thought to have many beneficial properties including making the baby content and to sleep more. After 40 days those who could afford it gave sweetened cow's or goat's milk but the poor who could not afford milk gave sweetened water until the child was 3–4 months old. Despite the fact that the sugar purchased in the market was covered with flies, it was considered a pure food that could not be polluted. For premature babies it was considered imperative that they were given palm sugar and anything else apart from this and breast milk was thought to be very bad for them. Mothers who could not afford to buy milk sometimes substituted what they call 'barley', a very thin porridge made with arrowroot. The greatest hardship for mothers was when they could not afford to sweeten this food. Highly sweetened food was given until the child was able to eat rice and tocari (sauce) but this was often not before the child could walk. It was believed that if this food were given earlier than this the child would have fits of anger or an upset stomach.

Rice was considered a 'strong' food and Hindu babies were first fed rice and rice derived foods only when nine months old at a rite called 'mukhebhat'. If the baby need supplementary food before that age rice would not be given but banana, biscuits, barley, tapioca or wheat products would be offered. Muslims also considered it to be dangerous to feed a child rice too early.

While almost every woman breastfed her baby and her ability to nurture her baby in this way was an important part of her identity, exclusive breastfeeding was not prevalent. This began with giving pre-lacteal food, instead of colostrum, with various supplements being given once breastfeeding had commenced. Formula was extremely expensive and beyond the reach of most of this group and much of the animal milk used was either diluted or infected. Although much of this feeding behaviour derived from traditional patterns, it seemed that the median duration of breastfeeding was significantly shorter than in previous reports from this country.

In a study which looked at breastfeeding in a number of different socioeconomic groups in Pakistan (Ashraf et al, 1993), the increasing use of formula, especially in economically advantaged groups, was very evident. Exclusive breastfeeding was uncommon as overall only nine per cent of babies were being exclusively breastfed at one month of age. Amongst the upper middle class no mothers practised exclusive breastfeeding. The most exclusively breastfed infants were found in the group from a rural village, but even here only 18 per cent were doing so. There was a rapid decline in exclusive breastfeeding in infants aged 1–3 months, although proportions depended on the season of the year. With an increase in temperature, fewer babies were exclusively breastfed whatever their age because they were more likely to be given extra fluids, usually water. In poorer areas, maternal milk with extra water was the preferred form of infant feeding. At one month, two thirds (64 per cent) of upper middle class mothers and 42 per cent of mothers from urban slum areas had started supplementary bottle feeds. At the same age 22 per cent in villages, and 12 per cent in periurban slum areas had started doing so, these lower figures presumably arising from the mother's inaccessibility to these supplementary foods, either because of lack of money or access to them in the shops.

During the first six months those initially fed only water were given animal milk or commercial formula with or without semi solids. This change happened earlier in urban areas, at around two months, than in rural areas independent of economic background. At six months of age 60 per cent of those from the urban slum, 52 per cent from the village, 42 per cent from the periurban slum and 39 per cent of the upper middle class were giving supplements of other milk to their babies. At one month fresh animal milk was the preferred supplement by all groups apart from the upper middle class, 80 per cent of whom preferred and could afford to give their babies formula. The use of a bottle with which to give the baby additional fluid and food was prevalent in all areas, although in the village more mothers used a dropper or cotton wick to give their newborns pre-lacteal feeds. At the age of one month, 100 per cent of those from urban areas, 88 per cent in the peri-urban slum and 82 per cent in the village were fed some food and fluids in a bottle. By the age of six months all babies in the study were receiving some nourishment from a bottle. Despite the very widespread use of breastfeeding supplements, only seven per cent of all infants in the study received no breast milk at age one month, most of these being in the upper middle class group.

The different patterns of supplementation found in 'developing' and 'developed' countries and their effect on breastfeeding was explored in a study which looked at the feeding patterns of Turkish mothers in Stockholm and Istanbul (Kocturk and Zetterstrom, 1986). Weaning (severance from the breast) and exclusive breastfeeding rates in the two areas were significantly different which related to the differing patterns of supplementary feeding. During the first month, 23 per cent of immigrant mothers, compared to only nine per cent of Istanbul mothers, weaned their babies. Thereafter, weaning rates increased sharply for immigrant mothers, all of whom had weaned by 12 months compared to only nine per cent of Istanbul mothers. In Istanbul exclusive breastfeeding decreased in favour of mixed or supplemented breastfeeding. The supplementary food consumed by the Istanbul infants relied mainly on home made mixtures prepared with diluted sweetened milk and rice flour or starch, plain milk or yoghurt. Commercial breast milk substitutes were used only to a limited degree, if at all, during the first few weeks when the infant was introduced to supplementary feeding while all the semi solids were home made. In Stockholm mothers preferred a direct passage to weaning, giving their babies a diet which relied totally on commercial infant food. It was interesting to note, however, that in both places the most common reason for introducing complementary feeding was that the mother felt she had insufficient milk. In Istanbul giving food to supplement breast milk did not necessarily lead to a cessation of breastfeeding, whereas in Stockholm it did. In common with other immigrant groups, however, the behaviour of these immigrant Turkish women conformed closely to Swedish mothers of similar background.

The results of these studies, which show long duration of breastfeeding with early supplementation, challenge many ideas about supplementary feeding and its effect on breastfeeding. In particular it seems that supplementation per se does not necessarily lead to either less initiation of breastfeeding, shorter duration or apparently any diminution in the volume of breast milk consumed. Why should early supplementation in developed countries lead to less breastfeeding while in less developed countries it does not? It has been argued that mothers in traditional communities are able to breastfeed for long periods even when giving their babies supplements, because their babies continue to breastfeed freely at night. This keeps up the level of the hormone prolactin which is essential for breast milk production. From this brief survey it appears that giving a baby formula from a bottle does seem to shorten breastfeeding duration in a way that traditional supplements do not. It is unlikely, however, that this comes about only because of physiological reasons with the baby having problems sucking at the breast once having sucked from a bottle. There are major lifestyle differences between those mothers who use formula and those who do not. Usually mothers who can afford the high cost of formula, and for whom it is easily available, live in urban areas. Here, there is likely to be an environment which is much less supportive of breastfeeding, especially if mothers go out to work in non-traditional forms of employment. It is interesting to note that in both urban and rural, developed and less developed countries, 'insufficient milk' is the most often given reason for supplementing breast milk. It would seem, however, that the way a mother deals with this – using formula or traditional supplements – has a great effect on whether or not she continues to breastfeed.

CHAPTER EIGHT

Breastfeeding Conflicts and Ambiguities

In traditional communities, pregnancy and birth are normal processes central to a woman's life and identity. A woman will marry, give birth and bring up children which, like the seasons of the year, is the natural progression of a female life. It does not follow, however, that for such women the process of birth and breastfeeding are free from ambiguity and conflict. In many traditions birth is surrounded by notions of pollution as well as power. A woman giving birth is both lauded for her strength and energy in giving birth, while at the same time being seen as a polluted person who must be excluded from normal life. In many traditional communities, as in the west, mothering carries many conflicting requirements. A mother may be judged as morally and spiritually inadequate on the basis not only of her own behaviour and health, but also that of her child. Breastfeeding and the perceived quality of the breast milk may be the focus of such conflicts and ambiguities which, if not negotiated successfully, can prove to be serious impediments to successful breastfeeding.

Our bodies, our place

The question of why childbirth is associated with pollution in India and how this might have come about has been examined in some detail by Janet Chawla (1994). Interestingly she begins her analysis by looking at ancient myths about female malevolent spirits in India and other cultures which, she says, express a general denigration of the experiences of women's bodies in patriarchal societies. The northern Indian version of this spirit is called the 'churel' and is generally thought of as the unsatisfied ghost of a woman who dies in childbirth. She is very beautiful and lures young men to their death with her sexual wiles and has devastating effects on women during pregnancy and childbirth. She is very powerful and is pictured with hands and feet pointing backwards, reflecting perhaps an image of an independent woman which is the exact opposite of an ideal woman in ordinary life where gender norms are quite different. In traditional Indian society the social value of women is narrowly defined in the roles of wife and mother. Such independence and autonomy has little expression and is often feared.

There are few, if any, references to traditional midwifery in the historical and sacred texts and this can be explained by a gender and caste bias which has devalued and even 'demonized' this group of women. In ancient times, women's bodily experiences were belittled by a powerful priestly caste which demonized certain female energies, while idealizing patriarchal motherhood and wifely chastity. Female blood, the sign of these female processes, was depicted as powerful, and often malevolently so. The blood of menstruation and birth was depicted as the site of extreme ritual impurity equated with death. The distinctly female work of birth was rendered by the priestly class as demonic and dirty and those connected with it, in particular the Dai, or traditional midwife, were considered outside the pale of religion. Originally such women came from a caste that was considered too polluted to enter a temple. This process has been so powerful that even now many women still believe in these judgements. There are other traditions which act as a counterpoint to these ideas and stress the auspiciousness and increase in prosperity which birth signifies, but as Janet Chawla points out, such ideas are expressed in the masculine voice.

How do such ideas affect the work of the Dai and how birth is experienced? Talking about pregnancy and birth with mothers from a less well-off urban community in Delhi, Janet Chawla found they greatly appreciated the Dai's 'hands-on' practical experience and knowledge of childbirth. The Dai's real importance and value to these mothers, however, was in her role as a ritual specialist. During the altered state of consciousness that mothers encountered during labour and birth, the Dai acted as an 'experiential guide' using ritual and sympathetic magic to help the mother make sense of, and go through, the experience successfully. The Dai was central to a women's labour and birth experience with rites that were exclusive to women, involving as it did ceremonies which were not part of the overall male centred religion.

Within this totally female environment, the Dai was not perceived as demonic and polluted. In fact she was perceived as an empowering force who occupied an important place in the cultural world of these Indian mothers. Her practices reaffirmed the special power of women to give birth and the bonds women created between them to do this. As such she created a strong counterpoint to the male dominated religion, which perceived these activities as producing extreme pollution. Despite such positive experiences of birth, women continued to feel ambiguous about their bodies. They were perceived as both possessing great power (to give birth) but at the same time creating pollution which set them apart from normal society and which were expressed in many of the exclusion rites in the 40 days after birth. This included a ritual (described in Chapter 5), a part of which was to remove the pollution of birth, so that breastfeeding could proceed without problems.

Birth may be considered polluting, but usually the period of pollution is thought to last only for a limited time and its effects are eventually neutralized by certain rituals. When such ideas carry over to breastfeeding, it can make the process a highly charged and equivocal activity which puts many restraints on the mother. This happens in Yemen (Beckerleg, 1991), where women live in a male dominated Muslim society and where ideas about women, childbirth and pollution give rise to ambiguities in how women feel about themselves and their bodies. Islam, as it is practised in Yemen, attributes women with a strong but destructive sex life. Women's sexuality is considered a powerful force which must be contained and controlled for the good of society as whole. Traditionally women were excluded from commerce and public with the home as their sphere and domain. They were excluded from the male sphere not because they were powerless, but because their power needed to be controlled and contained. Women and men thus live very separate lives, with women creating a world of their own within the domestic sphere to gain greater power and autonomy over their own lives. In this society women and men inhabit separate worlds.

Spiritually women are considered below men; sex, menstruation and childbirth are thought polluting, so many women perceive their bodies as powerful yet polluted and as a potential source of disorder. Sex is considered healthy and normal but only when contained and controlled within marriage and surrounded by ritual precautions. Childbirth further pollutes women and sets them apart from their husbands as all men are banished from the house during labour and delivery. They feel as if they are in an indeterminate situation which leaves them feeling generally vulnerable and uncertain about themselves as women. This is exacerbated for most women by their heavy workload and repeated pregnancies, which often results in poor health. Not surprisingly this carries over to the process of breastfeeding which, as a process intimately connected with female body cycles, has aspects which are dangerous and ambiguous. Breastfeeding is seen as an activity, which although good, is difficult to achieve successfully. It is hedged around with restrictions (already described in Chapter 5) to ensure that the breast milk is good and does not cause problems for the baby. A mother must always be on her guard to prevent her activities from adversely affecting her breast milk.

In Bangladesh (Blanchet, 1991), similarly equivocal ideas about the nature of women and their place in society were part of the discourse about breastfeeding and affected how it was perceived and conducted. For the Bangladeshi mothers in this study, their ability to breastfeed successfully was an important part of their identity, and failure to breastfeed was out of the question. Babies were thought to have a right to the breast which, as well as providing nutrition, was also used as a pacifier and a way of getting babies off to sleep. The ability to breastfeed had both positive and negative aspects which were related to two different, and sometimes contradictory, discourses on the inherent qualities of men and women. The most often heard was that a wife's body, sexuality and breast milk belonged to her husband who was also her master. This was acknowledged when women discussed the use of contraceptives as to do this she had to get permission from her husband. Within this context, the qualities of women most often praised were obedience and devotion to her husband, regardless of whether or not he was a good provider. At the same time wives had positive qualities and a unique power which was to make things grow through their nurturance and devoted care. This was signified in the idea of the 'lukkhis' who was an ideal wife who managed the household granary, nurtured the child in her womb, breastfed her baby and saw to its growth. In addition she looked after the wealth of men and her qualities were such that she helped them be wealthy and prosperous. Men on their own could not become prosperous but needed this nurturing energy from women to do so.

The powers of the 'lukkhi' were associated with the rice economy and the traditional subsistence farming rather than the money economy. At the time this research took place, the money economy was gaining in importance and it seemed that, as a result, the value of women's activities was decreasing. This could be seen in the changes that had come about in marriage payments. Such payments used to be made from the man's family to that of the woman in recognition of the loss of the woman's work and power in her family. As the importance of the women's contribution has decreased, however, and women are considered more of a liability than an asset, payments are now made from the family of the woman to that of the man. Maybe these changes and devaluing of the woman's contribution were associated with the increasing belief that breast milk on its own was inadequate.

Women expected that as they had more children, their health would deteriorate. Their nurturing role was expected to be carried out regardless of what they ate and, if necessary, at the expense of their own health. This was particularly true during the Ramadan fast when women, whether pregnant or lactating, were supposed to be more pure and, by keeping the fast more religiously than their men folk, benefit the whole family. They had a special responsibility to fast just because they were responsible for their children and their men folk. Food which was highly valued and nutritious, such as milk and eggs, was often given to children and men rather than the pregnant mother. Women had been socialized to do this to such an extent that if there was food on her plate and her child asked for it she felt duty bound to give it to the child. Women who were given a boiled egg at the antenatal clinic had to be given it to eat out of sight of their children. Breastfeeding was part of this depleting process, which a woman expected to undertake on behalf of her children but for which she was receiving less and less positive acknowledgement.

The idea of mothers being totally self-sacrificing is also true amongst mothers in Mexico (Millard and Graham, 1984), where pregnancy, birth and breastfeeding are seen as a process that involves maternal sacrifice for the sake of the child. Pregnancy obligates a woman to restrict her diet and social activities and birth is considered a potentially life threatening event that is the most physically painful of all experiences. As a result, all children are considered to owe their mothers a debt of gratitude because of her self-sacrifice. This debt is increased with lactation, as breastfeeding is thought of as draining some of the bodily substances from a woman. It is not acknowledged to be pleasurable for a mother, although it is for a child. A child is thought to have to repay the mother for these sacrifices when she reaches old age and needs to be cared for. At the same time, however, birth and breastfeeding are a focus of both knowledge and power for women. In observing lactational precautions and regimens, women have considerable autonomy. Women and family members counsel one another but the mother is always considered the ultimate authority and decision maker with regard to her child. The power of women to give birth and the autonomy they have with regard to child rearing is tempered by the self-sacrifice that it also entails.

Our bodies, our breasts

In our modern western society, ambiguities about breastfeeding often focus on the breast and its strong sexual connotations, as well as infant feeding potential. From a biological perspective (Dettwyler, 1995), human females have breasts for nurturing their children, but from the cultural perspective breasts and breastfeeding can have many other meanings. It surprised a researcher to find that in Mali breasts have no sexual connotations either for men or women. Women in this community found it difficult to believe that men could become sexually aroused by breasts or that women could find sexual activities with their breasts pleasurable. Are breasts intrinsically erotic? The author thinks not and that the perceived eroticism of breasts is learned behaviour in exactly the same way that the tiny bound feet of Chinese women were considered the ultimate in erotic stimulants. She compares the practice of foot binding – taking a perfectly healthy functional organ and mutilating it into something only for male sexual pleasure – with that of breast augmentation surgery in the US which is undertaken for exactly the same reasons.

Breasts play no role in sexual behaviour in any other species except humans and evidence does not support the idea that male attraction to breasts is widespread. A cross-cultural survey of patterns of sexual behaviour was carried out in 190 cultures around the world (Ford and Beach, 1951), and it was found that in only 13 out of 190 were breasts viewed by men as erotic. The size and types of breasts considered erotic varied considerably. In only 13 cultures were women's breasts stimulated before or during intercourse, only three of which were also listed among the 13 where breasts were considered sexually attractive. From this evidence it would suggest that American (Western?) men have learned to find breasts sexually stimulating as Chinese men learned to be sexually stimulated by a woman's small feet.

It is not surprising that in such a cultural context, where breasts have become highly sexualized, many people are not comfortable seeing a woman breastfeeding. In the US many women have been told in various public places, such as restaurants, that they must not breastfeed. There are many examples of women who have been arrested, fired from their jobs or harassed simply because they were breastfeeding outside their homes. In a national advice column, women were advised only to breastfeed in private or, if they have to feed the baby in public, to pump out their milk at home and give it to their babies in a bottle while they were out. Other ideas which reinforce such attitudes are that breastfeeding serves only a nutritional function, is only for young infants and should only be carried out in private. Such a culture against breastfeeding puts enormous constraints on any woman who wishes to do so and it is small wonder that so few women either initiate or continue to breastfeed in the weeks and months after birth.

Such cultural constraints on breastfeeding and ambiguous feelings about breasts are but one aspect of the complex and subtle things that influence women deciding on how they should feed their babies. Statistical associations between such factors as age, education and socio economic status to breastfeeding are much less straightforward than the figures imply, as Pamela Carter (1995) found in a group of women of various ages and backgrounds in the north of England. The decision to breast or bottle feed was a complex one. Women's experience of their bodies and the sexualization of their breast were but two factors which they had to negotiate in trying to find a feeding pattern which suited both themselves and their babies.

Asked about how they felt about breastfeeding, these women found it difficult to name and evaluate the sensations they felt, these being an uncomfortable mixture of those that 'belonged' to mothering and those that 'belonged' to sex. This was hardly surprising in view of what Carter calls the conflicting discourses around breasts. Increasingly breasts have become the constant object of male gaze with particular kinds of breasts signalling to men female attractiveness and approval. At the same time women have to keep their breasts respectable but 'attractive' which means having to cover or uncover them at appropriate times. To be respectable means that your breasts can only be looked at by the right person, at the right time, for the correct purposes. It is not just a matter of time, place and viewer, however, as different kinds of breasts (size, shape and colour) have different meanings and signal different things to men. A woman must be attractive and desirable but she must also be respectable which means controlled in the extent to which she covers and uncovers her body, in particular her breasts.

At the same time, if she is a mother, her children must be nourished and nurtured and uncovering her breasts to do this often arouses contradictory messages and feelings. This was especially so if, within her living area, she had no private space in which to breastfeed or felt that she had to remove herself completely from everyone else in the household. Of those able to express feelings only a few women were able openly to express enjoyable sensual feelings around breastfeeding. Those who breastfed often had stronger and more equivocal feelings and such contradictions were one important element in whether mothers decided to feed their babies with breast or bottle. Not surprisingly many women found it easier to bottle feed which was not hedged around with such contradictions and ambiguities, was not connected with their bodies in such an intimate way and did not therefore give rise to such disturbing feelings.

Breastfeeding and men

In many traditional communities men do not take an active part in childbirth and are often, but not always, excluded from the act of giving birth. This is not to say, however, that they have no role and in no society is a man absolved completely from action which will help his wife give birth. Although he may be excluded from the birth, he may have to carry out crucial rituals sometimes during the pregnancy and often connected with the disposal of the placenta. If his wife has problems during labour, the father may be called to participate in rituals that will facilitate the birth. In the literature about breastfeeding in traditional societies, there is little mention of men in this respect, although as I described in the first chapter, if a Zimbabwean mother has problems breastfeeding her baby, a ritual confession of adultery by the father will be enough to get things started again.

Breastfeeding, like birth, is in many traditional communities considered the domain of women. Some of the immigrant women in Carter's study spoke with nostalgia about their experience of breastfeeding in their own countries compared to what they had experienced in the UK. In their own countries there was less medicalization of childbirth and a greater knowledge of breastfeeding within families. Women were much more likely to have seen their female family members breastfeeding before they did so themselves and other women were role models and a source of knowledge, help and support. With a greater separation between the sexes, there was more physical space just for women where they could create their own social environment for breastfeeding. It was felt that the loss of such space was one reason that made breastfeeding much more difficult for these mothers within the UK.

In the last 20 years in the west, men have become more and more involved with childbirth. In the 1950s a father's attendance at birth was radical behaviour. By the 1970s it was commonplace and by the 1980s it was expected behaviour. From the father's point of view this has had both positive and negative effects. Some men have found that it deepens their relationship with their wives but for others it has been a deeply disturbing experience with negative effects on the couple's subsequent relationship (O'Driscoll, 1994). Fathers have also been encouraged to participate more in the care of the newborn baby, but for some when the baby is being breastfed this is problematic. A number of studies (Voss, 1993; Gamble and Morse, 1993; Jordan and Wall, 1990) have shown how many fathers feel excluded from the breastfeeding relationship and the various strategies that they adopt to deal with this. It is not surprising that one of the most important factors determining whether a woman will decide to breastfeed or not is the attitude of her partner.

Another factor of considerable importance, which research has uncovered and which was a considerable surprise to me, was the large proportions of men in the west who feel that breastfeeding should not be a public activity. In a survey carried out by the Royal Society of Midwives in the UK (News Focus, 1993), half of the men surveyed objected to women breastfeeding 'in any place they chose'. They commented that breastfeeding was embarrassing, unnecessary, a form of exhibitionism, attracted attention or was disgusting behaviour. Similar results were found in a survey of fathers carried out in Houston (USA) (Hoelscher, 1993) where a much greater proportion of the fathers (70 per cent) felt that breastfeeding in public was not acceptable. As the authors point out, it is unlikely that such a large proportion of fathers would claim that it is unacceptable to wear bathing suits in public, an act which often exposes more of a woman's breasts that breastfeeding. This, of course, shows a response to the ambiguities about breasts from the male point of view. It may also be felt by them as deeply disturbing as it challenges their 'ownership' of women's breasts, both individually and culturally. This author goes on to describe how breastfeeding can be 'discrete', carried out in the right way with the right clothes and so there is no reason for a woman to be put off by such attitudes. I feel that it is more pertinent to ask about the kind of society we have where the views of men on this are not questioned. Maybe it is a case of men needing to be re-educated, rather than women having to wear special clothes or curtail their activities just so that men don't get upset.

It would be interesting to know about the attitudes of men to breastfeeding in traditional society, but to my knowledge no-one has carried out any research on this subject. Certainly in some communities men are considered to 'own' the breast milk so that, in theory, if a woman wishes to stop breastfeeding she has to do so in consultation with her husband. In many traditional communities men and women live more separate lives after birth to the extent that a breastfeeding mother may have little to do with her husband while she is breastfeeding. In some African polygamous communities, the time of birth and breastfeeding will be a period when a mother devotes herself entirely to her child and she will not have sexual relations with her husband. Where a trend towards monogamy has made this more difficult, it can have negative consequences for the health of both mother and child.

Sometimes, however, a woman's behaviour with regard to infant nutrition derives and reflects wider gender inequalities which are exacerbated by modern 'development' (Maher, 1992). The increasing involvement of rural societies in the cash economy has often led to a shrinkage in the subsistence sector, which is usually the responsibility of women and a corresponding increase in the economic power of men. This brings into sharp relief the dependent status of women and the fact that their access to land and cash is often mediated by men. Cash, in many developing countries, is controlled by men and spent according to their wishes rather than the needs of the family. In many communities the role of the father is associated with authority and privilege rather than nurturing behaviour. Boys are not usually socialized to assume caretaking roles in relation to women and children but rather to enjoy privileges at their expense. This is very evident when it comes to intra-familial food distribution where it is common for women to be the last to eat and to have whatever is left over from the men and children, which in most cases is not the most nutritious food.

Where women have lost control over their own means of subsistence, transferring to men some of the costs of baby care, through bottle feeding, is one way of coping. This is particularly so in situations where women are doing this work all alone on an ever slimmer budget of food, cash and vitality. Bottle feeding can represent an element of self-preservation, as in doing so women give up the impossible task of compensating with their own bodies for the shortcomings of an environment which is hostile to women and children. Where they are increasingly devalued for their breastfeeding and other subsistence work, bottle feeding is a way to get men to take over some of the responsibility for child support. In this situation to suggest that breastfeeding constitutes a saving to the national economy is to ignore the worsening situation of women and children. By breastfeeding, women will make things even worse for themselves.

Putting men under pressure to purchase tinned milk for their children and recognize and take responsibility for them was evident in Caroline Bledsoe's work (1995) on the meaning of 'tinned milk' among the Mende of Sierra Leone (West Africa). In this community mothers chose to give their babies tinned milk for reasons related to their economic dependence on men which made it necessary for them to side step the postpartum taboo on sex. Among the Mende the semen of a man other than the father was thought to be harmful to a breastfeeding baby. To prevent accusations of causing a child's illness from breast milk contaminated by semen, mothers weaned their child on to tinned milk at a very young age. As well as avoiding the accusation that a child's malnutrition could be attributed to the woman's resumption of sexual activity, the male provision of tinned milk was a public sign that the man acknowledged paternity. For economic security, women had to ally themselves with men and did so partly through sexual relations. Giving a very young baby tinned milk allowed a women to resume sexual relations and thus reinforce the ties she had with the baby's father. At the same time she obtained public acknowledgement and financial support from the father which strengthened ties between mother, father and child.

Insufficient milk

Physiologically speaking it is has been estimated that only a very few women are physically incapable of breastfeeding. Even malnourished women have enough breast milk to breastfeed successfully, although they may do so at the expense of their own bodies and health. Yet in many research studies carried out in all parts of the world a significant reason for mothers ceasing to breastfeed and start using a breast milk substitute is that they have 'insufficient milk'. For this reason it has been the subject of intense debate, although this has not always been particularly well-informed, especially when the influence of traditional and modern lifestyles on breastfeeding have been discussed.

The so-called 'insufficient milk syndrome' (Gussler and Briesemeister, 1980; Greiner, Van Esterik and Latham, 1981), is the name given to a pattern of influences which stop women breastfeeding successfully and lead them to believe they do not have an adequate supply of breast milk. It is described as deriving from 'modern' urban lifestyles where, as birth has become more medicalized, babies are not continuously kept close to their mothers, who as a result, become less tuned-in to them. Babies must therefore cry longer and harder to let their needs be known and the times between feeds becomes longer. Breasts will be more full and the more hungry babies will suck harder and longer making nipple pain more likely. With increased crying the mother's anxiety will be raised and her 'let down' reflex will be impaired. This sets up a vicious circle which interrupts the physical breastfeeding process. When breasts are more full and nipples sore and the mother's 'let down' process impaired, the baby cannot obtain the necessary quantity and quality of milk. This leads to insufficient nipple stimulation and the production of less breast milk, which increases the baby's hunger and crying and further disturbs the breast milk production and feeding cycle. This might be reinforced by health professionals who undermine a mother's confidence in her ability to breastfeed; by the advertising of baby milk manufacturers that encourage mothers to interpret any problems as being due to insufficient milk, and by the difficulty that many mothers have in breastfeeding in public. The 'insufficient milk syndrome' is therefore said to derive from ways of living in modern industrial societies and urban areas of developing countries. This is compared to lifestyles in rural traditional societies which are presumed to be more compatible with successful breastfeeding and where, it is assumed quite wrongly, that insufficient breast milk is not a problem.

That insufficient milk could be a problem in traditional communities is acknowledged by the proliferation of traditional remedies to ensure the condition never arises. In the days immediately following birth, mothers are often given special food which is both for her rejuvenation and for ensuring a good milk supply. Banana flowers are given to mothers in Southeast Asia and peanuts in Zimbabwe. In Yemen (Beckerleg, 1991), great concern was expressed about insufficient milk and certain food, such as chives and sorghum porridge, were mentioned as foods good for increasing milk supply. In Papua New Guinea (Whiteman, 1965), Chimbu mothers considered sugar cane to be of great value. In cases of insufficient milk the husband should bring sugar cane for his wife to eat. Amele mothers (Jenkins, Orr-Ewing and Heywood, 1984), also in Papua New Guinea, steamed their breasts over a cooking pot if they felt that their milk supply was failing.

As was described in Chapter Six, breast milk is a powerful yet mysterious substance with physical and non-physical attributes affected by both material and non-material influences. Mexican mothers (Skeel and Good, 1988) knew that inadequate nutrition decreased milk production so tried to eat more, but they were also careful about cold on their body which could dry up their milk. They covered their shoulders, especially at night, did not walk barefoot on the floor and were careful with the cool air from an open refrigerator. In Guatemala (Solien de Gonzalez, 1963), non-physical reasons for insufficient milk included nervousness, unhappiness, fright and sickness such as fever or stomach problems. At the same time it was thought to be related to the quality and quantity of foods that a mother ate and there was a general agreement that if a mother needed to produce more milk, she should drink more milk herself. Three plants were mentioned as milk fortifiers which could be taken either as a prophylactic or treatment. As has already been described, insufficient milk can also be the result of supernatural forces deriving from conscious or unconscious envy and jealousy from other women or from unsatisfied ghosts of women who died in childbirth.

Insufficient milk is also not always just a matter of having a sufficient quantity of breast milk. In Mithila, for instance, a crying baby was considered to be not only hungry but also mentally dissatisfied. Breastfeeding was, therefore, a way of restoring contentment to a baby as well as providing nourishment. The mother's ability to satisfy this demand, however, was thought to depend on her being able to produce a regular abundant supply of 'full' milk. A mother who had 'full milk' not only had breasts that were producing to full capacity but was also producing milk which nourished the baby and provided contentment and satisfaction as well. The ultimate measure of the 'fullness' of the breast milk was the mother's ability to satisfy her baby which also showed that she was a successful mother, with the right moral and emotional relationship with her infant.

This subjective measure of the baby's contentment was easily distorted, however, by maternal feelings of inadequacy. If the baby was not developing into a plump, playful and somewhat demanding toddler, mothers often assumed that their milk was deficient, insufficient or unsuitable. She might try to improve things by taking over-the-counter allopathic or Ayurvedic tonics or by supplementing her breast milk with milk formula, or more likely the cheaper barley water. If the problem was thought to lie with the infant, tonics for the baby would be purchased to give the child an appetite and enhance digestion. Many women complained of being 'weak' and this medicalized a problem stemming from the hard work they had to undertake on behalf of their mother-in-law. Such 'weakness' was thought to come from constant strain, overwork, malnourishment, childbirth and loss of blood in menstruation. It could also, of course, be the symptom of other illnesses and very probably anaemia. Whatever the cause, 'weakness' featured as a legitimate excuse for avoiding certain tasks and a breastfeeding mother suffering from this was unable to produce full milk. Unless she resorted to bottle feeding, the infant could become listless and grow only slowly.

As this research from Mithila shows, perceived problems with insufficient milk can be a focus for a mother's insecurities concerning her ability to feed her baby adequately. It can also be a potent way of bringing attention to her problems and legitimize action that she takes to improve her situation, such as taking extra rest which she might not otherwise feel justified in doing. This was also evident amongst breastfeeding mothers in Turin (Italy); several mothers had problems acknowledging the strong feelings they felt about their baby's crying as it went against the accepted principle that a mother should have unqualified love for her baby. In this situation a mother might find it easier to justify herself by saying that the crying stemmed from her milk that was inadequate, rather than that she could not hold out against the baby's crying to maintain a breastfeeding schedule. Thus the perceived shortcomings of the mother were projected onto her breast milk. To plead 'insufficient milk' was one way of disentangling oneself from the cultural imperative that 'breast is best' and that one should be breastfeeding. It was an acceptable way of not breastfeeding but, as the authors point out, at the cost of giving the breastfeeding a mother a negative image of herself.

The concept of insufficient milk is, therefore, a complex one with many different layers of meaning which will vary in different cultural contexts. In traditional communities, insufficient milk may derive from many non-physical causes which include ghosts, witchcraft, envy and jealousy as well as local conditions like a cold wind on the shoulders. Women may feel that they have a lack of breast milk for various reasons and this lack may be in quality as much as quantity, although the breast milk will still be described as 'insufficient'. Perceived feelings of having insufficient milk may be a way of drawing attention to an unsupportive environment and can legitimate a mother's demands for less work or for her husband to spend more cash on the baby's food. Other reasons may relate to deeper feelings about her adequacy as a mother or ambiguity about her body. Deciding that she has insufficient milk and therefore not to breastfeed may be a way of handling these conflicts by using a much less emotionally charged method of infant nutrition.

As the concept and perception of insufficient milk varies, so will the things that need to be done to help mothers deal with it. Often it is assumed that when mothers understand the physical basis of breast milk production, then simple measures such as encouraging them to allow the baby to suck more will be sufficient. Such a biomedically oriented solution may, however, be quite inappropriate. Where insufficient milk is the result of non-physical factors, such as witchcraft, rituals and other spiritual practices are more appropriate and successful. If a mother believes that her breast milk is insufficient because of the work of ghosts or witches, she will not expect a solution that focuses on the physical process to be successful. Exhorting mothers to allow their babies to suck more to build up their breast milk supplies will not be effective with mothers already undernourished and living in unsupported environments. Seeing it as a problem that can be solved by individual actions of women is to worsen their situation even more. In such situations it is political changes that are needed to empower and provide more equitable resources for women and children.

CHAPTER NINE

The Transition to Adult Food

'Weaning' is a rather loose term used to signify both the introduction of solid food to the baby's diet, as well as when the baby stops breastfeeding completely. These are, however, different processes and I use 'weaning' to indicate the introduction of solid food, and 'severage' the time when a baby stops breastfeeding. How a baby makes the transition from a diet consisting entirely of breast milk to that of adult food is a diverse process both within and across cultures. Communities usually have general ideas about how this weaning and severage should proceed, but it is subject to considerable variation in individual cases for a wide range of practical and attitudinal reasons.

When the breastfeeding has to stop: severage

In many traditional communities one of the most common reasons which mothers give for stopping breastfeeding is that she has become pregnant again. There are various ideas about the effects this might have on both the unborn child and the breastfeeding infant and consequently why a mother should not try to continue breastfeeding. In the Philippines (Fernandez and Guthrie, 1984), for instance, when a breastfeeding mother becomes pregnant it is thought there are two infants competing for milk which is only sufficient for one. One of the two could therefore sicken and die and since the unborn child is considered more vulnerable, the older one is usually weaned to give both infants a better chance of survival. Amongst those mothers who do continue breastfeeding despite pregnancy, an episode of diarrhoea in the older child is a sign that the milk is not good and that breastfeeding should be discontinued.

A new pregnancy was one of the most common reasons for weaning an older child in Guatemala. Here it is thought that the breast milk of a pregnant mother will make the older child sick with stomach cramps and diarrhoea. The unborn child might also suffer if the older child is 'sucking all the milk'. Despite these beliefs, a few women ignore these taboos and breastfeed throughout pregnancy showing that, even when there are strong beliefs about this, mothers can still exhibit considerable autonomy. After the birth of the new child, however, the older child ceases to be breastfed. Amele mothers in Papua New Guinea are also forced to hurry up weaning if they become pregnant again. As few know, however, that they are pregnant before three months, most mothers continue to breastfeed until their pregnancy is clearly visible to all. It is widely believed that a child who suckles while a mother is pregnant is drinking the blood of the new sibling which will coagulate in the stomach of the older child to form a swollen belly. The acceptable period of birth spacing is two years between babies and should a child be forced from the breast before this period, it is known as a child 'sent from the breast too soon'. This too has negative effects on the older child who could develop a swollen belly from having to eat 'strong foods' too early. The distress of early weaners is obvious and mothers come under severe criticism if this happens, partly because by becoming pregnant she has obviously ignored the taboo against having sexual relations while breastfeeding.

In this community there was great variation at the age at which severage took place, the most quoted 'ideal time' being between 12 and 18 months. There was no criticism, however, for weaning a child anywhere between nine months and two years. A new pregnancy was the most usual reason for severage, but other reasons for weaning (especially by those who did so at 12 months) include the idea that longer nursing would make the child naughty, cause nosebleeds or give the child a disagreeable character. No relationship was found between either age of mother and age at weaning or economic status and breastfeeding. Women who travelled more outside the village and had more contact with doctors and western medicine tended to wean earlier. The final severage is accomplished by refusing the breast to the child. Each time the child cries he or she is offered a cup, bottle or piece of food. It was reported that although the child cried bitterly for a few days, they soon forgot. Sometimes mothers put bitter material on their nipples to discourage the child. At the same time, however, the delicacy of the weaning period is recognized in that the child is never harshly treated or spanked during this time.

In Mithila a two-year period between first and second child was considered optimum but if a mother became pregnant after only one year, the negative effects were on the toddler not on the unborn baby. When the mother was pregnant and breastfeeding, the unborn baby would 'eat' from the blood first so that the resulting milk was deficient in nourishment. The unborn baby had normal growth but the toddler did not. By the fifth or sixth month, it was thought that the breast milk became salty causing the toddler to lose interest and, as a result, to become 'dried out' and weak. Salt was associated with poison as it was used by witches to put on the lips of babies to make them sicken and die.

In many traditional communities, another very common reason for discontinuing breastfeeding is through illness of the mother. If the mother is very ill immediately after giving birth, this is one of the situations in which the baby in a traditional community may never be breastfed – at least by its mother. In the Guatemalan research it was found that of three children never breastfed, one had a cleft lip and two were unable to breastfeed as the mother was sick with fever soon after birth. In the 11 cases where children were weaned under nine months (the lowest 'normal' age for weaning) in all but one case, where the mother was working, it was because of sickness of the mother. The idea that a mother should discontinue breastfeeding if she became ill was also found in a study in India (Chandrashekar, 1985). Here 41 per cent of mothers thought they should stop breastfeeding if they had diarrhoea, 38 per cent if they had cough and fever, 8 per cent if they had a cold. It was, however, unclear whether mothers expected to discontinue breastfeeding completely or just for the duration of the illness.

The idea that if a baby is ill, breastfeeding should be stopped for the duration of the illness is a tenacious one in many communities. I have experienced myself the devastating effects it can have on babies when used as 'cure' for diarrhoea or malaria and the baby becomes dehydrated and eventually dies. The research in India found that such ideas were still prevalent with 26 per cent of mothers believing they should stop breastfeeding if the baby had diarrhoea, 10.7 per cent in the case of a cough and 1.3 per cent in the case of a cold. A large number said that any illness of the child would get worse if breastfeeding continued. Again it was unclear whether mothers considered that breastfeeding should cease completely, but in many places this is all too common and babies are denied nourishment just when they most need it.

The weaning process

As previously discussed in Chapter Seven, in many communities around the world solid food of various sorts is introduced to the baby very soon after birth. The baby thus has a mixed solid food and breast milk diet for a long period before breastfeeding stops completely. In many communities, although such solid food is given, breast milk is a very important source of nutrition, maybe the only source of protein, especially when the solid foods are not high in nutritional value.

The character of the first solid food and when it is introduced can be subject to a number of ideas about the nature of a baby's body and what he or she can eat at different ages. As previously mentioned, in Peru (Wellin, 1955) a baby's body is thought to grow in a particular way and must be prepared at each stage of growth for the ingestion of different sorts of food. As described in Chapter Seven, during early infancy until some time before the sixth and twelfth month, the child receives only milk except for herb tea or sugared water. The first supplement that a child receives will probably be animal milk given in a bottle. This fulfils a number of needs. It permits the breastfeeding mother occasional freedom of movement, allows her to withhold the breast when she is ill or has violated a food prohibition and, perhaps most importantly, it accustoms the child to the bottle well before he or she is to be taken from the breast. Unfortunately this researcher did not investigate in detail the diets of infants as they made the transition from breast milk to adult food, except to say that the child was gradually initiated into different sorts of food according to how the mother perceived the strength of the baby's body to receive it.

In Guatemala (Solien de Gonzalez, 1963), a child must be deemed as being able to 'eat well' before starting to eat solid food which, in practice, means that the infant should have at least four teeth. This is said to happen some time between the eighth and twelfth month of age. In this community, mothers distinguish between 'gruel', 'food' and 'fruit'. Gruel can be given to small infants of only a few months of age, but food, which includes bread, tortilla, beans, rice, vegetables and meat is considered not suitable for infants until they have teeth. In the earliest stages of weaning small pieces of soft food are given for the child to try out and if anything seems to disagree with them, this is withheld until the child is 2–3 years old. Bananas are usually the first fruit given to a small child even before the teeth have come through, but once the child has teeth other fruit are freely eaten. Usually children are given whatever food they can chew by themselves, and by time there are enough teeth to chew well (at the age of two or thereabouts) then the child is normally eating the same diet as adults.

Sometimes, however, the stages through which a child passes as it grows up and the food appropriate to each stage is more precisely delineated. The Amele in Papua New Guinea (Jenkins, Orr-Ewing and Heywood, 1984) have a sophisticated system of named stages through which a baby passes. At each stage, certain sorts of food, according to their system of food classification, are thought to be particularly appropriate. In the Amele diet, the principle staple foods are taro, bananas and yams, with coconuts being very important and providing the major source of fat. During the rainy season, when taro and yams are unavailable, people depend on a variety of other starchy food such as bananas, Chinese taro, 'pitpit', winged beans, sago, corn, cucumbers, pumpkin, sweet potatoes, manioc and, increasingly, imported rice. In addition to these staples, a small amount of animal protein is consumed and there are a wide variety of green leafy vegetables available, some of which are high in protein. An economy with an increasing emphasis on earning cash, rather than subsistence agriculture, has brought about an increased consumption of a variety of different food bought from the store which includes tinned meat and fish, as well as rice. Fruit and nuts, including the breadfruit seed and peanuts, are important and nutritious snacks.

The Amele classify their food in different ways. One classification is according to their source and different qualities. Food known as 'saab' refers to major staples and anything annually grown in the garden, 'ehiro' includes fruit, nuts growing on trees and vines, while 'uhun' (meat) from 'dor' (animals) includes mammals, lizards, fish, birds, eggs, crustaceans and insects. Each variety of food is further classified as 'strong', 'soft', 'hot' or 'cold'. The quality of strength is widely recognized and subsumed other characteristics such as hardness, density, stringiness and dryness. 'Strong' foods are considered inappropriate for young children without teeth and sick persons. Watery foods, such as juice and broth, represent the extreme of softness and are thought excellent for infants. Food can also be classified as hot or cold but this system is less widely known and is explicitly taught only to special people. Heat is associated with life and potency, cold with weakness and death. Physiological states, including states of development and body fluids, are classified as hot or cold, this indicating the type of food or medicinal plant required to balance the hot or cold state and restore harmony to the body. According to this classification, infants are thought to be in somewhat of a cold state and so therefore need warm, soft, watery food.

Child development is marked through a series of specifically named changes in motor development and tooth eruption and each stage is thought to require a change in diet. Newborn infants ('momodo') are cold and soft like their mothers and as the baby's strength increases and the infant lifts up his or her head, he or she is known as 'momo memen'. There is a subclass of food which is considered appropriate for these very young infants. Such items are distinguishable by their high moisture content and include semi-liquid mashed ripe banana, and papaya often cooked in water, broth of pumpkin and sweet potatoes. When the baby is able to sit, he or she is known as 'biberen' and this is a major step as at this point it is thought the baby is ready to eat mashed foods. The infant is, however, considered too young to eat strong, dry foods or very cold foods which are usually identified by being slimy and bloody. Food cooked in coconut milk, a very common way of cooking in this community, is thought to be somewhat slimy and therefore unsuitable for a child of this age.

A child who crawls is called 'o'o'obona' (meaning 'he walks like a pig') and the first sign of standing is greeted with joy by fathers who build crossbars for their children to help them stand and walk. At this stage, when the children also have some teeth, many are given some food of animal origin – usually fish. When a child walks by him or herself holding onto a bar or onto a parent, he or she is called 'da'a'en'. At this stage many regularly eat some meat, most have tasted eggs and all eat the Amele staples. A child at this stage can eat food cooked in coconut milk without harm. When able to walk, without holding on, the child is called 'ji o'obona' ('he walks the road') and 'gudugudu'ena' when able to run about, play with other children and ask for food. By this time any kind of food can be given to the child who eats more or less the same as adults.

Dental eruption was also used as a guide but the stages were much less well defined. Three types of teeth were recognized: incisors, canine and 'cheek teeth'. There was considerable variability between respondents concerning which sorts of food could and could not be given when particular teeth appeared. In general, however, parents agreed that it was permissible to give food cooked in coconut milk (a major part of the adult diet) when at least two incisors appeared and sago and meat when the cheek teeth appeared.

Traditional weaning amongst African Pokot mothers (O'Dempsey, 1988) is also very gradual. The first non-breast milk food which is given to young babies is diluted animal milk which is diluted less and less as the child grows older, thus providing more and more nourishment. A mixed diet is introduced when the child is old enough to reach and take food from the mother's plate, although meat is not given until the child is about two years old as it is believed to cause fever and ill health if given when the child is too young. Similar weaning patterns are found in Zanzibar where weaning foods consisting of porridge made of millet, maize or rice flour are given at age 2–4 months. From the age of six months, mashed potatoes, soft rice with a few vegetables are given and gradually the child eats more and more solid food until the child no longer needs and refuses to breastfeed. Weaning also happens gradually in Mithila in India (Reissland and Burghart, 1988), starting when the baby is about six months old. By one year the baby is actively encouraged to eat solid foods, although breast milk is available on demand until the baby's third year. Should the mother no longer wish to suckle the baby she rubs her breasts with crushed margosa leaves, the bitter taste causing the child to reject the breast.

Weaning and severage is not always, however, a gradual process. In Mali (Dettwyler, 1987) there is a wide range of ages in weaning but the process is fairly uniform. The mother chooses a day to wean and the child is not allowed to breastfeed from then on. Mothers talked about substances they could put on their nipples to discourage their child but no mothers in the sample actually did this. At the time of severage, women wear clothes that cover up their breasts so the child finds it hard to get to them. Sometimes the child is left with a friend or relative or the mother goes away. Extra food is given to the child to make up for the breast milk and to help them forget. Milk and fish, or meat, are the most common foods given to a child who has just been weaned. Giving extra porridge, cough syrup and just walking about with the child on her back are other things a mother might do to help her child over this period. For the great majority of children, despite the seeming severity of the method, severage does not seem to be an emotional trauma. In the sample only two children showed evidence of being upset about it. There was a general feeling that children ate more after ceasing breastfeeding, as most children seemed to prefer to breastfeed, while breast milk was available, than to eat solid food.

Most of the mothers in this sample had emigrated from different parts of the country to the urban slum where the research took place. They represented a range of different ideas and practices from various other parts of the nation and had various beliefs about weaning which affected the weaning process. The introduction of solid food into the infant's diet was carried out by most mothers when the infant was around six months of age but it could happen anywhere from three to 24 months. Mothers reported little or no decline of nursing with this introduction of solid food. Anecdotal evidence from mothers suggested that in the villages from which they came, children stopped breastfeeding when they wanted to do so, usually between two and three years of age. Despite this, most mothers in the sample said that infants should stop at 24 months but those who wanted to do so later gave village practice as evidence that this had no harmful effects. A reason given for not continuing to breastfeed after 24 months was that the 'child will become stupid'. Women accept this as 'urban wisdom', together with the idea that at around that age breast milk is not needed by the child. Data on 78 children in the sample showed that the mean age of weaning was 20.8 months, that nearly two-thirds (63.4 per cent) of children weaned between the ages of 18 and 24 months and this was very similar for both boys and girls. Birth order positively correlated with weaning, older children being weaned at younger ages than younger ones.

The most common reason given (by 45 per cent of mothers) for severage was that the child was 'old enough' as defined by age or growth of the child. If the child asked for the breast, this was considered to be an indication that he or she was old enough to stop breastfeeding. A few children became disinterested in the breast and more or less severed themselves. Pregnancy was also a very common reason for severage. With the breakdown of postpartum sex taboos in this urban area, the gap between pregnancies was getting shorter and as a result many children were stopped from breastfeeding before 24 months. Eighteen (24 per cent) of the sample stopped breastfeeding for this reason with a mean age of 16.5 months. The health implications of this are very significant; mothers have more pregnancies closer together and the youngest child loses many months of the extra protein from breast milk. The mother had to 'decide' she was pregnant, however, and would do this anywhere between one and five months of pregnancy. Some six children in the sample stopped breastfeeding because their mother became sick, a further six because the child was sick, three of whom showed better health after severage had taken place. Some five children stopped breastfeeding themselves and four children were encouraged to stop because their mother was tired of breastfeeding them. In only two cases did severage take place because of perceived insufficient breast milk and in one case the mother went back to work when her child was six months old.

In Mexico (Millard and Graham, 1984) it is also thought that severage should happen quite quickly as a mixed diet of breast milk and other food is thought to weaken the child. Traditional 'rules' about weaning and severage do not stipulate a correct chronological age but depend on the child's physical and behavioural development as perceived by the mother. The 'rules' are therefore not to be followed blindly but require judgement. It is thought, for instance, that once a child has teeth, breastfeeding should finish as it shows that the child is mature enough to eat normal food. This 'rule' allows considerable latitude, however, as teeth start coming at six months and finish at 18 months or more, so severage at any time during that period is considered alright. It is also thought that breastfeeding should cease before the child is too mature, otherwise the child will become boorish and ill-mannered, but the exact time is decided by the mother. In one village, researchers found that women stopped breastfeeding on average when the child was ten months old, whereas in another village breastfeeding stopped at 20 months. In the former village, women were closer to western medicine and said that doctors encouraged them to introduce breast milk substitutes and stop breastfeeding earlier than was traditional. In this village there was a greater incidence of hospital births with several women commenting that the medicine they received during birth contaminated their breast milk. The researchers thought that this was one reason why 16 per cent of the women they spoke to from this village did not breastfeed at all.

Data about child mortality and weaning were collected in both villages. This showed that children's ages at death suggested major peaks in mortality associated with severage and the subsequent withdrawal of breast milk. A number of children died at the average age at which supplementation of breast milk was reported and there was another peak in mortality when breastfeeding stopped. The researchers were quick to point out, however, that it was not necessarily traditional patterns of weaning and severage that were at fault, as weaning foods were not necessarily nutritionally inadequate. Poverty also significantly correlated with child mortality so these peaks in mortality may have been related to that, rather than nutritionally inadequate food.

As this, and other research in developing countries has shown, the period of weaning, when a child is changing from a diet of mainly breast milk to one of ordinary food, is often a time of some risk. This is particularly the case when weaning foods are not high in nutritional value. In Malawi, for instance, I found the most popular weaning food was maize porridge, maize being the staple which was considered to be very strengthening. Unfortunately, however, the capacity of a child's stomach was rarely large enough for the child to eat sufficient maize porridge for its nutritional needs. For this reason children often became thin and ill if subsisting on a diet of porridge with no breast milk. A local hospital dealt with this problem by giving mothers a 'weaning food' consisting of ground maize and soya flour. This greatly increased the nutritional value of the porridge with the advantage that it was prepared and looked exactly the same as ordinary maize porridge and so was very acceptable to mothers.

In India there are a wide variety of weaning foods such as rice and ragi porridge. On their own they are usually insufficient to ensure the proper nutrition of the just weaned child, again because of the large quantity that needs to be consumed to obtain sufficient nourishment. An easy and acceptable way of increasing the nutritional value of such food is to add small amounts of ghee (clarified butter) or oil which is also used in adult food. In one Indian study (Chandrashekar, 1985) it was found, however, that only 21 per cent of mothers in the sample were doing this. What was perhaps rather disturbing was that as the level of literacy and education of the mother increased, a greater proportion of them neither knew about, nor used, oil in weaning food. In fact many of the most educated mothers thought that the best weaning foods came from a tin, suggesting that the advertising messages of commercial companies were getting through rather more successfully than that of health professionals.

The low nutritional value of weaning food was one of the explanations given for the large numbers of underweight Amele children in Papua New Guinea. During the first six months of life, breast milk appeared adequate in three-quarters (77 per cent) of children, while for the rest, who were losing weight, neither breast milk alone or in combination with other food was adequate. An analysis of the food given to a sample of babies at this stage showed that this was probably because 91 per cent of it was water, since warm liquids were considered the most appropriate food for infants at this stage of development. As well as having little food value, it is possible that the high liquid content filled up the small stomachs of the infants to the extent that it limited the amounts of breast milk they were able to ingest. Most children (82 per cent) between the age of six and 12 months lost weight on a diet that was highly dependent on breast milk. When children began to crawl, their growth faltered with nearly half (45 per cent) with weight that levelled off somewhat below the average standard. One reason for this may have been because the extra activity of crawling increased their energy requirements. Just over one-third (35 per cent) continued to gain weight relative to the standard at this age while 20 per cent continued to lose weight. This pattern was exacerbated by the indulgent child rearing patterns in this community. Mothers did not persist in offering supplementary foods and in fact children were not given either the breast or other food for which they had not asked.

Reducing the risk associated with weaning, as this research shows, requires some understanding of how the weaning process is perceived by mothers. In particular, as in the case of the Amele, local ideas about the nature of a baby's body, the stages through which it passes and the food appropriate to each stage need to be understood. Only then is it possible to suggest ways, such as improving the nutritional quality of weaning food, to make weaning less risky to children and which will be acceptable to mothers and their families. It is also extremely important not to discount the effects of poverty on the diets of young children as very often it is this, rather than traditional weaning practices per se, which causes the problem. Any programme aimed at improving the nutrition of young children has to address and take action against this often more intractable problem as well.

An appropriate time to wean?

One of the main differences between traditional and modern weaning patterns is that the latter takes place much earlier than the former. It is evident that mothers living in developing countries (usually in urban areas), who have been more exposed to modern medicine and probably with more money and access to a better diet, tend to wean their babies earlier. This was shown in research carried out in India (Katiyar, 1981), where mothers living in rural areas were later in introducing solids and later in completing weaning or severage from the breast than those in urban areas. Two-thirds (66 per cent) of middle class urban mothers had weaned their baby before six months compared with just under half (40 per cent) of those in the urban slum and only 23 per cent of mothers in rural areas. Half of urban children first received solids at 7–12 months of age but urban slum and rural children were first given solids much later, at between 13 and 18 months of age.

Common weaning foods in all groups were sago, rice and dal, mashed potato and green vegetables, while the more expensive eggs, rice and curd were more often given by mothers in the middle class urban group. Infants from the urban slum and rural areas were much later than those in the urban group in having an adult diet. One reason for this was that mothers in these areas believed that certain food such as cereals, meat, curd, brinjal, jackfruit and root vegetables, if fed to their infant, would result in liver disorders and distension of the stomach. It was, therefore, common practice not to allow children to have these things until they were deemed old enough to resist their harmful effects. By contrast, the majority (83 per cent) of urban infants were allowed, and even encouraged, to eat anything.

It is difficult to see where modern biomedical ideas about the optimum age at weaning came from, although attitudes concerning the extent to which babies should be 'indulged' (or not) by breastfeeding for long periods might have something to do with it. In the US, for example (Dettwyler, 1995), paediatric 'rules of thumb' suggest that weaning should take place either when the birthweight triples or that the period of breastfeeding should be equivalent to that of gestation. Is there a physical basis for these suggestions? One way of determining whether there is a physiological basis for such suggestions is to look at the weaning periods of primates, such as gorilla and chimpanzee, whose genetic makeup is most similar to humans. Various criteria can be used to identify the average time at which such primates weaned their young. This includes: weaning according to reaching one-third adult weight, according to adult body size, according to gestation length and timing of eruption of the first permanent molar. It appears that if humans were weaned only according to these physical criteria, then severage 'should' take place in humans when the infant is between two and a half and seven years of age. It therefore seems that the extended breastfeeding seen in many traditional communities is more in line with our biological heritage than the early weaning times seen in countries like the US.

This might appear to be of merely of academic interest to those of us in the west whose children have access to breast milk substitutes, a nutritious diet and for whom weaning is rarely a time of risk as it can be for those in less developed countries. It does, however, have other implications for health professionals and parents. There have been various court cases, for instance, which have involved charges of abuse when children are breastfed as toddlers. Extended breastfeeding has been used against mothers in court battles over child custody where 'failure to wean in a timely manner' has been used as evidence of a mother's unsuitability as a parent when in fact such a mother may be more in tune with her biological heritage. Given the usually unfavourable response to extended breastfeeding in the US, it is not surprising that mothers breastfeeding older infants usually do so in private.

CHAPTER TEN

Breastfeeding and Infant Nutrition – The Wider Picture

Writing about traditional patterns of infant feeding is, I have found, rather like making a patchwork quilt, with many different pieces which can be fitted together in various ways. As a patchwork quilt can be viewed from different perspectives from which other, and sometimes unexpected, patterns can be seen, so looking at the way we feed our babies within a wider context can show unexpected things about what we think and do. It can help us to appreciate the diversity of ideas and behaviour about infant feeding, of which our own style is but one, as well as pointing us towards positive possibilities for the future.

The mirror of society

Ideas about infant feeding are connected with a multiplicity of ideas, attitudes and cultural mores. Sometimes they can be seen to be closely related to traditions of birth. Sometimes it is more appropriate to view them in connection with traditional ways of viewing the body and ideas about digestion and health. Very often such traditions reflect different economic realities, power relationships between men and women and a particular concept of what it means to be a woman. They may also reflect spiritual ideas about the place of humans within the wider universe. Frequently concepts of infant feeding do not form a coherent whole and there may be different, and sometimes contradictory, ways of looking at it. Different parts of a community or members of a family may view and explain infant feeding in different ways. Mothers themselves may be more or less conscious of conflicts and contradiction which have their focus on ideas about how they should or should not feed their babies. Patterns of infant feeding are a mirror for the community in which they take place.

How do we choose how we feed our babies? While there are a great many statistical studies, there is much less which explores such choices from the women's point of view. Such research as there is shows that the choices that women make about infant feeding are not just about choosing to breast or bottle feed. They are a complex negotiation on many different levels between a mother and all the different demands made upon her. These are not only practical demands but ideological ones concerning the nature of woman and how she is supposed to be as a mother. I feel further inquiries of this nature would be of considerable use in highlighting the enormous stress under which many women live their lives. This would be particularly so in places where they are only marginally nourished and where there are accelerating economic and other changes, which devalue the contribution of women and in which the traditions that once supported them no longer do so.

Further investigation about the perception of 'insufficient milk' would, I think, be particularly relevant and insightful, but only if it was carried out in a way that uncovered the subtle constraints which mitigate against women's autonomy and lack of choice in infant feeding. Such an inquiry would not be merely an academic exercise or part of a Government programme to impose yet more constraints on women. It would be firmly grounded in women's experience and practical realities. It would be the basis for making positive and profound changes that enable women to make really autonomous choices, not only about how they feed their babies, but how they live their lives.

Different perspectives on birth and breastfeeding

In traditional communities, ideas and ways of feeding the newborn are intimately connected with traditions associated with pregnancy, labour and birth. They are perceived as normal processes where emotional and spiritual, as well as physical, forces are at work. This is reflected in the many traditions and rituals to harness emotional and spiritual forces, as well as physical ones. A woman, generally with the help of other women and maybe traditional midwives, uses various methods to work in harmony with these forces rather than trying to control them. Traditions of infant feeding recognize emotional and spiritual aspects, as well as acknowledging various family ties between the newborn, the rest of the family and through that the wider community.

By contrast, in the west, pregnancy, labour and birth are perceived as mainly physical processes that are not an ordinary part of life but conditions which require medical surveillance and assistance. The body is thought of as similar to a machine which during pregnancy and birth is expected to conform to certain patterns. The biomedical view of birth is that such processes can and should be controlled. While giving birth, a woman may not be 'allowed' to labour for more than a certain number of hours or 'push' beyond a certain length of time before it is deemed that intervention is necessary. It is expected that breastfeeding mothers will require some kind of medical assistance even though in hospitals, where birth normally takes place, this is not always forthcoming. Nowadays women are not expected to breastfeed according to an externally imposed schedule but, as the survey of the paediatric literature showed, the clock is still very much part of paediatric advice. Babies, like everyone else in modern societies, are expected to conform to some kind of regular schedule and if they do not do this it is cause for comment.

Despite these problems with the biomedical approach to breastfeeding, there is a growing body of physically based research which could herald profound changes about how we perceive and help women breastfeed. A research study from Sweden for instance (Righard and Alade, 1990), demonstrated the very strong instinctual processes which, if left undisturbed, allow breastfeeding to happen seemingly effortlessly immediately after birth. Two groups of newborns were compared: in one group babies were removed from their mother's abdomen 20 minutes after birth and in the other contact was uninterrupted for at least one hour. In the contact group, after about 20 minutes, infants began to make crawling movements towards the breast, the rooting reflex soon came into play and at an average of 50 minutes after birth most of the infants were suckling at the breast. Most infants in the contact group showed the correct sucking technique. Also of interest was that of the 26 infants who did not suck, 25 were born to mothers sedated with pethidine. This research, with its very detailed observations, shows the wonderful interrelated physical reflexes by which the baby, if not disrupted by external forces, is enabled to breastfeed successfully.

Speaking from the point of view of a practising obstetrician, Michel Odent (1992) has described how he has many times seen the instinctive patterns of the newborn baby and mother which, if not disturbed, will culminate in breastfeeding. The newborn instinctively knows how to find the nipple and the mother knows how to coordinate her own behaviour with her newborns so that breastfeeding takes place at the right time. If a mother is in a private situation where she is free to tune into her own instinctive processes, this will happen on its own. Just as she was able to surrender to the energies that enabled her to give birth, she can surrender to the subtle interplay between mother and newborn that make breastfeeding possible. In such a situation a mother does not 'put the baby to the breast', but rather coordinates her actions with that of her baby so that the baby can suckle. Michel Odent believes that the important thing is to create a private space for mother and baby where they can become attuned to each other and not to disrupt the process.

Unfortunately, however, such knowledge has not been widely translated into positive action in terms of creating the kind of environment where this can happen. It is true that many hospitals in the UK now have a written policy about breastfeeding which acknowledges this research but the impact on newly delivered mothers is often not great. Findings from the Policy and Practice of Midwifery Study (Garforth and Garcia, 1989) showed, for instance, that in 43 observed deliveries where the mother had chosen to breastfeed, the average time before the baby started breastfeeding was 98 minutes after birth, but that it ranged from between one minute to 12 hours. In ten instances the first feed did not take place until more than two hours after birth. It seemed that examining and dressing the baby and other needs of the hospital organization often took precedence over establishing the relationship between mother and newborn. The special time immediately after birth, when both mother and baby are especially receptive to starting breastfeeding, was lost.

Nowadays mothers and babies in the west are not automatically separated at birth but there is still a tendency to view them as two separate individuals who are connected in rather mechanistic ways rather than as a symbiotic whole. The importance of mothers and babies just to be together and to 'tune into each other' on a number of levels is not recognized as they are in many traditional communities. As I have argued earlier, I think that one reason that mothers in traditional communities are able to deal with initial disruptions to the physical process of breastfeeding is because mother and baby are kept in close physical proximity away from the normal concerns of daily life. In the west, a similar recognition of the mother and baby relationship would be of particular help to those mothers and babies separated soon after birth, either through illness or because of having had a caesarean. A modern equivalent of the exclusion period (which Sheila Kitzinger calls the 'babymoon') to start as soon as mother and baby can be together would not only help to establish breastfeeding, but would also help such women to feel confident of themselves as mothers. As women need privacy to give birth, they also need privacy to establish this relationship especially in these special circumstances. Such a period of time would, for all women, be a time to recognize the total emotional and spiritual aspects of just having had a baby.

How shall we feed our babies?

However we feed our babies we often feel we have to do it 'right' by some external criteria. As the wider picture of infant feeding shows, however, there is not, in any absolute sense, a 'right' method. Data from traditional communities shows that infants can be fed in many different ways. In the west, advice about infant feeding has been inconsistent and gone through a series of metamorphoses since the beginning of the 20th century. Disturbingly, we are now realizing that much of this advice led to there being many more hungry babies. It may have contributed to the demise of breastfeeding, the long-term effects of which are only now becoming apparent (Stuart-Macadam, 1995).

Feeding our babies, especially if we breastfeed, is not just about getting food into babies. It has sensual, emotional, social and spiritual aspects, none of which are acknowledged by the biomedical model. One of the most important things which I think this study of these traditions reaffirmed is the holistic nature of the experience. I realized that many of the struggles I had feeding my first baby were brought about by the exclusive focus on the physical process. Breastfeeding was a series of manoeuvres to be learnt so that my baby ingested the right amount of food. The introduction of solids had to proceed in a certain way and severage should happen when my baby reached a certain age or weight. Only later did I feel that giving my baby food was also as an experience of love and communication. It was some time before I could allow myself to trust the relationship between myself and my baby through which we expressed and satisfied our needs for 'food' in the widest sense.

I think that to feed our babies we need to do less and attune more. We should attempt to develop with our babies a relationship of sensitivity whereby needs can be expressed and satisfied, and to have confidence that the 'right' way of feeding our babies will develop from this. The challenge for health professionals and for society as a whole is to find ways to support and empower mothers to do this. This needs, I feel, a fundamental shift in our thinking whereby mothers are valued not only for their practical contribution to infant feeding, but for the inner knowledge which they develop to do this successfully.

References

Ashraf, R.N. et al (1993). 'Early child health in Lahore, Pakistan v feeding patterns'. *Acta Paediatrica Supplement* 390, pp. 47–61.

Balsalmo, F. et al (1992). 'Production and pleasure; research on breast feeding in Turin'. In: Maher, V. (Ed). *The Anthropology of Breast Feeding – Natural Law or Social Construct.* Oxford: Berg.

Beckerleg, S. (1991). 'Socio religious factors affecting the breast feeding performance of women in the Yemen Arab Republic'. Personal communication.

Blanchet, T. (1991). 'An anthropological study of maternal health in Nasirnagar'. A Save the Children (USA) Impact Study carried out for a workshop on maternal health and neo-natal care.

Bledsoe, C.H. (1995). 'Side-stepping the postpartum sex taboo: Mende cultural perceptions of tinned milk in Sierra Leone'. Mentioned in: Dettwyler, K.A. 'Beauty and the breast: the cultural context of breastfeeding in the United States'. In: Stuart-Macadam, P., Dettwyler, K.A. (Eds). *Breastfeeding: Biocultural Perspectives.* New York: Aldine de Gruyer.

Carter, P. (1995). *Feminism Breasts and Breastfeeding.* Basingstoke: Macmillan.

Chalmers, B. (1990). 'Infant feeding practices amongst Pedi women'. *International Journal of Perinatal Studies*, pp. 69–80.

Chandrashekar, S. (1985). 'Infant feeding practices in a coastal area of Dakshina Kannada district'. Summary and conclusions of PhD thesis; personal communication.

Chawla, J. (1994). *Child Bearing and Culture – Woman Centred Revisioning of the Traditional Midwife: The Dai as a Ritual Practitioner.* New Delhi: Indian Social Institute.

Dettwyler, K.A. (1995). 'Beauty and the breast: the cultural context of breastfeeding in the United States'. In: Stuart-Macadam, P., Dettwyler, K. (Eds). *Breastfeeding; Biocultural Perspectives.* New York: de Gruyer.

Dettwyler, K.A. (1987). 'Breast feeding and weaning in Mali: cultural context and hard data'. *Social Science and Medicine*, 24, 8, pp. 633–44.

Dettwyler, K.A. (1995). 'A time to wean: the hominid blueprint for the natural age of weaning in modern human populations'. In: Stuart-Macadam, P., Dettwyler, K. (1995). *Breast Feeding; Biocultural Perspectives.* New York: de Gruyer.

Dreyghton, M.L. (1992). 'Breast feeding and baraka in northern Tunisia'. In: Maher, V. (Ed). *The Anthropology of Breast Feeding; Natural Law or Social Construct.* Oxford: Berg.

Enkin, M., Keirse, M.J.N., Renfrew, M.J., Neilson, J.P. (1996). *A Guide to Effective Care in Pregnancy and Childbirth.* Oxford: Oxford University Press.

Fernandez, E.L., Guthrie, G.M. (1984). 'Belief systems and breast feeding among the Filipino poor'. *Social Science and Medicine* 19, 9, pp. 991–95.

Fildes, V. (1986). *Breasts Bottles and Babies – A History of Infant Feeding.* Edinburgh: Edinburgh University Press.

Ford, C.S., Beach, F.A. (1951). *Patterns of Sexual Behaviour.* New York: Harper and Row.

Gamble, D., Morse, J.M. (1993). 'Fathers of breastfed infants: postponing and types of involvement'. *JOGNN* 22, 4, July/August.

Garforth, S., Garcia, J. (1989). 'Breast feeding policies in practice – no wonder they get confused'. *Midwifery* 5, pp. 75–83.

Greiner, T., Van Esterik, P., Latham, M.C. (1981). 'The insufficient milk syndrome: an alternative explanation'. *Medical Anthropology,* Spring.

Gunnlaugsson, G., Einarsdottir, J. (1993). 'Colostrum and ideas about bad milk – a case study from Guinea Bissau'. *Social Science and Medicine* 36, pp. 283–88.

Gussler, J.D., Briesemeister, L.H. (1980). 'The insufficient milk syndrome: a biocultural explanation'. *Medical Anthropology,* Spring.

Heyn, B. (1987). *Ayurvedic Medicine.* London: Thorsons.

Hoelscher, J.L. (1993). 'Making breastfeeding user friendly'. *IJCE* 8, 2, pp. 30–31.

Hull, V., Thapa, S., Pratomo, H. (1990). 'Breastfeeding in the modern health sector in Indonesia: the mother's perspective'. *Social Science and Medicine* 30, 5, pp. 625–33.

Jackson, D.A. et al (1992). 'Weaning practices and breast feeding duration in Northern Thailand'. *British Journal of Nutrition* 67, pp. 149–64.

Jenkins, C.L., Orr-Ewing, A.K., Heywood, P.F. (1984). 'Cultural aspects of early childhood growth and nutrition among the Amele of lowland Papua New Guinea'. *Ecology of Food and Nutrition,* 14, pp. 261–75.

Jordan, P.L., Wall, V.R. (1990). 'Breastfeeding and fathers: illuminating the darker side'. *Birth* 17, 4, December.

Katiyar, G.P. et al (1981). 'Feeding practices in Varanasi district'. *Indian Pediatrics* 18, January, pp. 65–71.

Khatib-Chahidi, J. (1992). 'Milk kinship in Shi'ite Islamic Iran'. In: Maher, V. (Ed). *The Anthropology of Breast Feeding – Natural Law or Social Contract.* Oxford: Berg.

King, J., Ashworth, A. (1987). 'Historical review of the changing pattern of infant feeding in developing countries: the case of Malaysia, the Caribbean, Nigeria and Zaire'. *Social Science and Medicine,* 25, 12, pp. 1307–20.

Kitzinger, S. (1987). *The Experience of Breastfeeding.* London: Penguin Books.

Kocturk, T., Zetterstrom, R. (1986). 'Breast feeding among Turkish mothers living in suburbs of Istanbul and Stockholm – a comparison'. *Acta Paediatrica Scandinavia* 75, pp. 216–21.

Kusin, J.A., Kardjati, S., van Steenbergen, W. (1985). 'Traditional infant feeding practices; right or wrong?'. *Social Science and Medicine* 21, 3, pp. 283–86.

Lad, V. (1993). *Ayurveda, the Science of Self Healing.* USA: Lotus Light Publications.

Maher, V. (1992). 'Breast-feeding and maternal depletion'. In: Maher, V. (Ed). *The Anthropology of Breastfeeding: Natural Law or Social Construct.* Oxford: Berg.

Millard, A.V. (1991). 'The place of the clock in pediatric advice; rationales, cultural themes and impediments to breast feeding'. *Social Science and Medicine,* 31, 2, pp. 211–21.

Millard, A.V., Graham, M.A. (1984). 'Breastfeeding and demography in two Mexican villages'. Working paper #48 on women in international development. Michigan State University, USA, April.

Muralidhar, P., Madhuri, M. 'Colostrum; evaluation from an Ayurvedic viewpoint'. Published in Marathi and translated by Surendra.

O'Dempsey, T.J.D. (1988). 'Traditional belief and practice among the Pokot people of Kenya with particular reference to mother and child health'. *Annals of Tropical Paediatrics* 8, pp. 125–34.

O'Driscoll, M. (1994). 'Midwives, childbirth and sexuality 2: men and sex'. *British Journal of Midwifery,* February, 2, p. 2.

Odent, M. (1992). *The Nature of Birth and Breast Feeding.* Westport: Bergin and Garvey Westport.

Panter-Brick, C. (1992). 'Working mothers in rural Nepal'. In: Maher, V. (Ed). *The Anthropology of Breast Feeding – Natural Law or Social Construct.* Oxford: Berg.

Radbill, S.X. (1981). 'Infant feeding through the ages'. *Clinical Paediatrics* 20, p. 10.

Reissland, N., Burghart, R. (1988). 'The quality of a mother's milk and the health of her child: beliefs and practices of the women of Mithila'. *Social Science and Medicine* 27, 5, pp. 461–69.

Righard, L., Alade, M.O. (1990). 'Effect of delivery room routines on success of first breast feed'. *Lancet,* 336, November, pp. 1105–106.

Royal College of Midwives (1988). *Successful Breastfeeding: A Practical Guide for Midwives and Others Supporting Breastfeeding Mothers.* London: RCM.

Salariya, E.M., Easton, P.M.,Cater, J.I. (1978). 'Duration of breast-feeding after early initiation and frequent feeding'. *Lancet,* November 25th.

Skeel, L.S., Good, M.E. (1988). 'Mexican cultural beliefs and breast feeding; a model for assessment and intervention'. *Journal of Human Lactation,* 4, p. 4.

Smale, M. (1992). *The National Childbirth Trust Book of Breast Feeding.* London: Vermilion.

Solien de Gonzalez, N.L. (1963). 'Some aspects of child bearing and child rearing in a Guatemalan ladino community'. *South Western Journal of Anthropology* 19, pp. 411–23.

Stuart-Macadam, P. (1995). 'Biocultural perspectives on breastfeeding'. In: Stuart-Macadam, P., Dettwyler, K.A. (Eds). *Breastfeeding; Biocultural Perspectives.* New York: de Gruyer.

Tieh Hee Hai Guan Koh (1981). 'Breast feeding among the Chinese in four countries'. *Journal of Tropical Paediatrics* 27, April.

van Steenbergen, W.M., Kusin, J.A., Kardjati, S., Renqvist, U.H. (1991). 'Nutritional transition during infancy in East Java, Indonesia; a longitudinal study of feeding patterns, breast milk intake and the consumption of additional foods'. *European Journal of Clinical Nutrition* 45, pp. 67–75.

Vasudevsastri, L. (1990). 'The neonate's first taking of breastmilk; Ayurvedic rationale'. Published in Marathi, translated by Surendra.

Vimala, V., Ratnaprabbha, C. (1987). 'Infant feeding practices among tribal groups in Andrah Pradesh'. *Indian Paediatrics* 24, pp. 907–910.

Vincent, P.J. (1991). *Birth without Doctors – Conversations with Traditional Midwives.* London: Earthscan.

Vincent, P.J. (1992). *Birth Traditions and Modern Pregnancy Care.* Shaftesbury: Element.

Voss, S. (1993). 'Fathers and breastfeeding: a pilot observational study'. *Journal of the Royal Society of Health,* August, pp. 176–78.

Wellin, E. (1955). 'Maternal and infant feeding practices in a Peruvian village'. *Journal of the American Dietetic Association* 31, September, pp. 889–94.

Whiteman, J. (1965). 'Customs and beliefs relating to food, nutrition and health in the Chimbu area'. *Tropical and Geographical Medicine* 17, pp. 301–16.

Woolridge, M.W., Baum, J.D. (1991). 'Infant appetite control and the regulation of the breast milk supply'. *Children's Hospital Quarterly* 3, p. 2.

THE BIRTH TRADITIONS SURVIVAL BANK

(Supported by the Department of Midwifery Studies, University of Central Lancashire, United Kingdom)

This was set up six years ago as a result of the first research I carried out on traditional midwifery. It seemed to me that birth traditions were fast disappearing and would vanish altogether unless some effort was made to document and keep them. The Bank consists of a computerized database of articles and books about world wide traditions associated with pregnancy, birth and infant nutrition. It also includes empirical data from research carried out specifically for the Bank and from women who have experienced various birth traditions either individually or professionally.

The aims of the Bank are:

- to bring together a wealth of diverse and scattered information about birth traditions world wide.
- to carry out empirical research on birth traditions before they are lost forever.
- to make this data accessible to everyone from pregnant women wanting to know about their own traditions to health care professionals or politicians wanting to integrate traditional practitioners into a woman-centred health service for women and children.

The Bank is in the process of making collections of articles on various relevant subjects which will be available in the near future. For further details of these write to:

Dr Priya Vincent
Adventure Community
Auroville 605101
Tamil Nadu
India

The Bank is always interested in hearing from anyone who, through experience or through their professional work, has come in contact with traditions old and new. If you have any information like this or if you are carrying out research on any relevant topic do please write and let me know about it.

Index